This book was released in a parallel universe before being released in this one.

To help the reader I would like to share comments from leading figures in that parallel universe.

*"I told everyone Felix was going to be trouble and see he was! If he and the Young Liberals hadn't stopped me at the Eastbourne Defence debate I'd have been Prime Minister!!! Well maybe David (Owen) would have been Prime Minister but I'd have shone his shoes EVERY day. I miss David (Owen) very much."* David Steel (former leader of the Liberal Party 1976-1988)

*"We should have given Felix that job at Social Democrat Party Headquarters instead of Danny"* Dr. Death (otherwise known as David Owen leader of the Social Democrat Party 1983-1987 [see letter from SDP page 58])

*"It will be my birthday on Tuesday. Last year, I reached the painful conclusion that there wasn't enough time left to read every book ever written. This year, my gloomy realisation is even more painful - I will not be able to correct everyone's mistakes before I depart. But with this book I'll make an exception."*
Daniel Finkelstein (Danny) former Chair of the Young Social Democrats and political adviser to the former Leader of the Opposition William Hague

*"We love Felix!! He is amazing. We buy all of his books – and so should you!"* Liberator (Liberal Party radical magazine)

*"Not everybody is comfortable with the idea that politics is a guilty addiction, but it is. I think this book shows that there is no such thing as paranoia. Your worst fears can come true at any moment."*
Dr. Hunter S. Thompson (gonzo journalist and President of the Young Liberals)

*"If you thought this book was frightening wait until Dodds writes the one about his time around the United Nations!!"* Michael Strauss (Executive Director of Earth Media)

# Liberalism in A Period of Change

# Confessions of a Young Liberal Activist 1975-1987

# By Felix Dodds

**Felix Dodds** was Chair of the National League of Young Liberals (1985-1987). He was also a member of the Liberal Party Council (1983-86). He has written or edited fifteen books the first of which was *'Into the Twenty-First Century: An Agenda for Political Realignment. (1988)'*. He was an Advisory Editor for New Democrat International (1988-1992). He is the President of Amber Valley Liberal Democrats.

Felix is currently a Senior Fellow at the Global Research Institute and a Senior Affiliate at the Water Institute at the University of North Carolina and an Associate Fellow at the Tellus Institute in Boston. He was the co-director of the 2014 Nexus Conference on Water, Food, Energy and Climate and will co-direct the 2018 Nexus Conference on Water, Food, Energy. In 2011 he chaired the United Nations Conference Sustainable Societies: Responsive Citizens.

His most recent books are *'Negotiating the Sustainable Development Goals: A transformational agenda for an insecure world'* (November 2016) written with the co-chair of the negotiations Ambassador David Donoghue and Jimena Leiva Roesch and *'The Water, Food, Energy and Climate Nexus'* (April 2016) edited with Jamie Bartram.

In December 2016 Comics Uniting Nations (UNICEF/PCI Media) published Felix's first comic: Santa's Green Christmas: Father Christmas battles Climate Change.

**Felix** was *Executive Director of Stakeholder Forum for a Sustainable Future* from 1992-2012. In 2011, Felix was listed as one of 25 environmentalists ahead of his time. (http://www.greenecoservices.com/25-environmentalists-ahead-of-their-time/)

# Contents

# Preface

On the 19th of May, 1898, the death was announced of Mr. Gladstone – four-time Liberal Prime Minister. Five years later, hopeful that Gladstone's legacy might be passed to a rising generation, the National League of Young Liberals was founded.

In the decades that followed, the Liberal Party experienced boom and bust, government and wilderness. Sometimes a powerhouse of ideas and a bastion of independence and conscience. The Liberal Party was also capable of being riven by factionalism, seeming irrelevant, and uncertain of where it fitted in the political landscape.

Yet, throughout bleak decades of endless electoral setbacks, the Young Liberals produced enough new blood to ensure that despite George Dangerfield's book, *The Strange Death of Liberal England*, the undertaker, the hearse and the coffin were never able to consign the corpse to the grave and that the obituary notices were premature.

In the post-war years, more than anyone else, from this Celtic Fringe Orcadian outpost, Jo Grimond breathed new life into the Liberal Party. Like a benevolent grandfather who knew exactly how to handle 1960s wayward grandchildren, he encouraged the National League of Young Liberals to explore the boundaries.

By the 1970s, their Red Guards were morphing into Green Guards and simultaneously engaging in community politics – sometimes in tough inner city neighbourhoods – and were never afraid to be a thorn in the flesh of the Party establishment.

In his racy, well-written and thought-provoking memoir, *Power to the People - Confessions of a Young Liberal Activist 1975-1987*, Felix Dodds provides an insightful sketch of the politics of those years and how the Young Liberals interacted among themselves, with the Party leadership, and how they responded to events.

We also learn a lot about Felix himself - not least his sometimes mischievous sense of humour – and about the clever band of young men and women who brought an untarnished, refreshing idealism and energy into the heart of political life. Some of them, like the late Mike Harskin, became an indispensable part of the Chief Whip's engine room. Others have gone on to make remarkable contributions in many walks of life.

Having cut my own teeth as a schoolboy chairman of the local branch of Young Liberals, a student Liberal activist, a Federation Chair during Peter Hain's time as National Chair, a Liverpool City Councillor at 21, National President of the Young Liberals in the 70s, and MP and Chief Whip in the 80s, Felix's narrative inevitably stirs many memories –

but you don't have to have been intimately involved in those times and events to learn something useful from this account.

In paraphrasing Samuel Ullman, Robert Kennedy once remarked that "youth is not a time of life, it's a temper of the will, a quality of the imagination." Perhaps this memoir is also meant to remind us never to stop trying to see things through younger eyes, nor to dismiss people or their ideas because they are young.

And ultimately, this memoir is all about passing on the baton – and a belief in the extraordinary privilege of living in a democratic and free society.

I do not know whether Felix Dodds is a relative of Elliott Dodds – who died in 1974, the year Felix's political feelings became aroused after attending a meeting about apartheid in South Africa – but Elliott Dodds would have been quite an inspiration for Felix.

In 1920, he published *Is Liberalism Dead?*, followed by six other major books between 1922 and 1966. Although he would not have agreed with all of Elliott Dodds' ideas, Felix would have recognised the clarity of his thinking and the importance of the Unservile State Group, of which, in 1953, Elliott became chairman, and which, for the first time since the publication of the Yellow Book, explored what British Liberalism was for in 1928.

Elliott Dodds came from the Nonconformist tradition, an ordained Deacon who, in common with many Liberals of his era, held faith and politics as one. He was a newspaper editor, journalist and publisher and insisted that Liberal parties "fail to go forward" when "Liberal thought remains hobbled."

Felix has been a worthy heir to this tradition – evident in his own writing, in the creation of the Young Liberal Philosophy Group, and a brave willingness to think outside the box. This hasn't always made him popular but, as his namesake rightly insisted, parties become hobbled and incapable of progress when they suffocate free thinking, crush conscience, or become incapable of accommodating or understanding dissent. From time to time, we all need to be challenged and made to feel uncomfortable.

There's an old saying that for the pearl to emerge from the oyster, a bit of grit has got to enter in.

In every generation, democracy and politics need more bits of grit. That's why this chronicle of the Young Liberals matters, and why Felix Dodds' story should encourage another generation to pick up that baton and to be part of an honourable tradition.

- David Alton

Lord Alton of Liverpool

Independent Crossbench Member of the House of Lords

www.davidalton.net

altond@parliament.uk

https://www.facebook.com/LordAltonofLiverpool

# Introduction

# My time with the Young Liberals

*"We are faced with the fact, my friends, that tomorrow is today. Procrastination is still the thief of time. Over the bleached bones and jumbled residues of numerous civilizations are written the pathetic words 'Too Late'."* Martin Luther King, Jr.

The Young Liberals have had a rich history. They were founded in 1903 and by the 1906 election had over three hundred branches across the country.

This short book is a story about my involvement in the Liberal Party but more accurately in the National League of Young Liberals (NLYL) in the 1970s and the 1980s. It shares my experience in being part of what became known as the *Green Guard*. I have written it as a story about the influence a group of young people can have on politics. I have tried to tell it as it was with all of our failures as well as our successes with our laughter and our sadness. I hope by doing so it is inspirational to you whatever your political persuasion.

My journey started by being inspired to engage in politics because of the challenge that John F. Kennedy gave in his inaugural speech in 1960:

*"Ask not what your country can do for you ask what you can do for your country."* I hope you will be too.

Underneath that is the belief that politics is a noble profession and that you could serve to make your country or your planet a better place to live in. This is something I deeply believe in. Best expressed with the Bobby Kennedy quote

*"Some people see things as they are and ask why? I dream of things that never were, and ask why not?"* (Kennedy, 1968)

I was fortunate to grow up in a stable middle-class family where we did discuss politics constructively. My father in particular, though a conservative, was keen that we debated the topics of the day. He was an example of someone who grew up in a working-class family, who did not go to university but ended up in the top management at Rolls Royce and then as Personal Director at the toy company Airfix. I guess in America it would be called living the 'American Dream'.

I have always been adventurous as a 16-year-old I hitched to Greece, as an 18-year-old I backpacked overland to Thailand. Just out of university and married to Rosie we took a year off for a honeymoon and travelled down the Nile to live and work in Khartoum as a teacher. The idea of exploring the world we live in has always excited me and if I had been born in a generation to come I would have searched out the stars to 'boldly go'.

The 1980s was a challenging time in British politics dominated by Margaret Thatcher in Britain and Ronald Reagan in the United States. It saw a resurgence in liberalism with the Liberal Party going into an Alliance with the newly formed Social Democrat Party (SDP).

It was also a decade of Militant Tendency battles in the Labour Party and a turn away from traditional 'One Nation' conservative policies in the Conservative Party as they embraced economic liberalism. It was a decade of peace marches against the placing of Trident and Cruise Missiles and anti-apartheid demonstrations outside the South African Embassy.

In our relaxing times we were listening to Madonna, Queen, Bon Jovi, Culture Club, Duran Duran, Tom Robinson, Bruce Springsteen, Sting, and Michael Jackson or we were listening to the new music of Punk – with the Stranglers, the Clash, the Jam, Blondie, Gang of Four, the Dead Kennedys and the Sex Pistols. Punk at times giving raw political messages. Punk was *"...primarily concerned with concepts such as pro-working-class, egalitarianism, humanitarianism, anti-nationalism, anti-authoritarianism, anti-corporatism, anti-war, anti-racism, anti-sexism, gender equality, racial equality, civil rights, animal rights, disability rights, free-thought and non-conformity. One of its main tenets was a rejection of mainstream, corporate mass culture and its values. It continued to evolve its ideology as the movement spread throughout North America from its origins in England and New York and embrace a range of anti-racist and anti-sexist belief systems."* (Wikipedia, Punk Ideologies)

In writing this book in 2017 I believe we live in perhaps the most insure world since the 1960s and what we need is inspired leadership that understands the risks and challenges ahead. Young people can take the lead in this.

Who would have ever guessed that we would see a President in the White House who doesn't accept science, and promotes fake news, who creates an even more 'Clear and Present Danger' to us all.

But I get ahead of myself. The greatest influence of the Liberal Party in the twentieth century was the 1906 to 1915 governments and the contribution to political thought that the Liberal Party of the 1930s had. It had an enormous impact on 20th century economic policy with the great thinkers of the time Keynes and Beveridge. I would remind the reader of a very relevant Beveridge quote:

*"Liberals believe our guiding force should not be self-interest, class conflict, but the determination not to rest while any are condemned to want, disease, ignorance and unemployment."*

Pretty good and still so relevant today! I would add to the end, `or an unsustainable planet`.

In the mid 2000's the Liberal Democrats were the only major political party that opposed the Iraqi war. They also predicted the economic crisis but DID not do enough while in government to break up the financial casino capitalism that still is prevalent in the markets. I raised my concern that this might happen over the environment too at a United Nations conference I was chairing in 2011:

*"In the same way that banks succeeded at privatizing the profits and socializing the losses as they led the global economy to the brink of collapse, we are in danger of doing the same with the environment. Humanity has taken a huge leap in the last decades and become a planetary-scale force - we need to behave as a global civilization if we are not to face catastrophic consequences."*

At the end of this book I reproduce a retrospective article I did for the Green Liberal Democrats in December 2017 for their magazine, Challenge. In this article, I wonder what I would do if engaging in the youth wing of today. What would be the issues I believe should be taken up and I built that narrative up through the enhanced Beveridge quote above.

I hope this book sparks some conversations in the Party and beyond. There have been two times where the Young Liberals have played a critical role in the philosophical direction of the Party. The first was of course the *Red Guard* period from the 1960s to the early 1970s. The second was the *Green Guard* in the 1980s.

The YLs of the *Red* and *Green Guard* periods were successful because they reached outside of the Party to bring new ideas and people into the Party but ultimately, they worked for the promotion of liberalism as opposed to the Party. It was a space for those on the left for freewheeling, free thinking, open mindedness – for those who were not dogmatic, interested in the pursuit of new ideas, and not afraid of controversy; for those always looking to update and refresh social liberalism. You can find liberals in all parties and that is why at the end of the *Green Guard* we produced the book *"Into the 21st Century: An Agenda for Political Realignment"* (1988) -still available on Amazon in which we argued we need to work on green and liberal issues across the parties together. An earlier echo of the talk of progressive alliances that are on the table now. By working together, I believe we can create a just, equitable, fair and sustainable planet that would be a great achievement for liberals.

A thanks to Patrick O'Hannigan and Tanner Glenn for editing. Louise Harris, Kieran Seale, Mark Jones, Graem Peters, Jane Brophy, Andrew Binns, Andrew Reynolds, David Campanale, Eela Dubey, Alexandra Coe, Lord David Alton and Michael Strauss for comments on the text, John Charles for the front cover and Dylan Harris for a photo. And a special thanks to my children Merri and Robin who I continue to have amazing adventures with.

Felix Dodds Apex February 2018

# Chapter 1

# The Beginning

*"And so, my fellow Americans, ask not what your country can do for you — ask what you can do for your country."*
John F. Kennedy Inaugural address, 1961

## Hemel Hempstead Young Liberals

I started to engage in politics while in the 6th form of school attending, though not yet joining, my local Young Liberal branch in Hemel Hempstead in Hertfordshire. Why the Young Liberals? I was inspired as I have said by the Kennedy brothers. *"Ask not what your country can do for you — ask what you can do for your country"*. The idea that we all should be in some way providing service to make the world, our country, our town or/and our community a better place has been at the core of my beliefs. John may have inspired the idea of service but it was his brother who I more identified with. Particularly Bobby's opposition to the war in Vietnam, his support for the civil rights movements in the US and in Northern Ireland. His clear internalization of what he saw in the poor neighborhoods he visited as Attorney General, as New York Senator or as a Presidential candidate.

*"It is a revolutionary world we live in. Governments repress their people; and millions are trapped in poverty while the nation grows rich; and wealth is lavished on armaments. For the fortunate among us, there is the temptation to follow the easy and familiar paths of personal ambition and financial success so grandly spread before those who enjoy the privilege of education. But that is not the road history has marked for us.*

*The future does not belong to those who are content with today, apathetic toward common problems and their fellow man alike. Rather it will belong to those who can blend vision, reason and courage in a personal commitment to the ideals and great enterprises of American society."* (Kennedy, 1968)

During the late 1960s and early 1970s, the Young Liberals had been at the forefront of the campaign in the UK against the South African Apartheid regime and the Vietnam War.

The chair of the Young Liberals was Peter Hain, a Kenyan who had been living with his parents in South Africa. They were active in the South African Liberal Party for which they had become 'banned people; briefly imprisoned and prevented from working. They left and moved to the UK. His mother and father, Adelaine and Walter Hain, I would meet later in my life when I was working for the United Nations Association. The Young Liberals had, with Peter's leadership, played a critical role in fighting for South Africa to be kicked out of international sport.

The issue of sport and apartheid had come to the forefront for most British people in 1968 with the proposed English cricket tour of South Africa. The England selectors chose as part of the England team Basil D'Oliveira, a South African 'coloured' man (according to the South African classification in place then) to tour with the team (In South Africa, people were then classified as Black, White, Indian, and Coloured). Only whites were allowed to play in the cricket leagues and the national side. South Africa's Prime Minister, John Vorster, attacked the selection saying:

*"It is not the MCC team. It's the team of the anti-apartheid movement."*

The tour was cancelled, but a 1970s tour of the UK by the South African Rugby team sparked massive demonstrations led by, among others, Peter Hain. Interestingly, the head of the Stop the 70s tour Glasgow group was future Prime Minister Gordon Brown.

South Africa was to be banned from international cricket and rugby and most sports by 1971 due to its apartheid regime. One of the books I still have on my shelf and which I quote often from is Peter Hain's "Don't Play with Apartheid".

The 1960s and early 1970s had been a period of protest, and throughout that protest, one of the guides to direct action had been Saul Alinsky's *"Rules of Radicals: A Pragmatic Primer for Realistic Radical's"*. The guide directed many future community organizing for new generations of radicals emerging from into the 1970s. One of the rules I liked was:

*"Power is not only what you have but what your enemy thinks you have".* (Alinsky, 1971)

**Alinsky's Rules for Radicals**

- RULE 1: "Power is not only what you have, but what the enemy thinks you have."
- RULE 2: "Never go outside the expertise of your people."
- RULE 3: "Whenever possible, go outside the expertise of the enemy."
- RULE 4: "Make the enemy live up to its own book of rules."
- RULE 5: "Ridicule is man's most potent weapon."
- RULE 6: "A good tactic is one your people enjoy."
- RULE 7: "A tactic that drags on too long becomes a drag."
- RULE 8: "Keep the pressure on. Never let up."

- RULE 9: "The threat is usually more terrifying than the thing itself."
- RULE 10: "If you push a negative hard enough, it will push through and become a positive."
- RULE 11: "The price of a successful attack is a constructive alternative."
- RULE 12: Pick the target, freeze it, personalize it, and polarize it." (Alinsky, 1971)

The story goes something like this.

A London University biology student was planning to wreck the 1970 South African Cricket Tour of the United Kingdom with an army of locusts. He announced that he already had 50,000 of the insects at his house and would have bred another 500,000 by the time the tourists had arrived for the match. The student, David Wilton Godberford, was quoted in The Times of London on 11th May as saying:

*"Anything up to 100,000 locusts will be let loose at a particular ground and I think the plan is foolproof. They will ravage every blade of grass and green foliage… So that their insatiable appetites will not be impaired they will not be fed for twenty-four hours before the moment of truth… It takes 70,000 hoppers twelve minutes to consume 50kgs of grass. The crack of a solid army of locusts feeding on the grass will sound like flames. The South Africans are going to dread this trip."* (Times, 1970)

There were no questions in the press about how you might breed 100,000 locusts in student accommodation. No questions about how they would be able to get them into the ground. The reason for this was all the previous actions taken by those in this campaign meant that this was treated as really possible or perhaps it was just that student rooms were bigger in those days.

On the 25th of September 1974, Peter Hain came to speak at my local Young Liberal branch in Hemel Hempstead on the Future of South Africa. The meeting was held in Hemel Hempstead School, and the meeting was packed. At the back of the Hall were the police who were clearly expecting problems. In their ranks was my local policeman from the village I lived in, Chipperfield. He was someone I knew well as he would come over for a drink with my father, and whose son I played cricket with on Chipperfield Common. Also attending the meeting was the National Front, a UK fascist organization that supported the idea of apartheid. As Peter spoke, these thugs threw bottles, eggs and chairs in his direction while we Young Liberals tried to protect him. The police did nothing to stop the National Front, and the meeting broke up. We took Peter out a back door. This had a profound impact on my views that there were freedoms we needed to protect and advocate for.

*"Liberalism is a political philosophy or worldview founded on ideas of liberty and equality. Liberals espouse a wide array of views depending on their understanding of these*

*principles, but generally they support ideas and programmes such as freedom of speech, freedom of the press, freedom of religion, free markets, civil rights, democratic societies, secular governments, gender equality and international cooperation."* (Wikipedia, 2017)

My involvement in local politics saw me active in the 1974 referendum on whether the UK should be in Europe. I was on the YES side and on the committee for Chipperfield' s campaign as I would have been if I was still living in the UK in 2016. I am a huge supporter of multilateralism and multilateral bodies as the best way to approach global or regional problems.

Chipperfield where I was living is situated between Watford and Hemel Hempstead in the commuter belt north of London. I attended Kings Langley Comprehensive School, which was only two miles from my house which was situated on a road called "The Street". A great name for a street! I loved the village. It was one of those English villages that you see in films. Very quaint, it had a wonderful common with a great cricket pitch and a wood that was so easy to get lost in. Not to mention that Peter Sellers lived for a period of time at Chipperfield Manor.

Overlooking the common was the Two Brewers Pub founded by Robert Waller as an ale house in 1799. It acquired fame as the place for 19th-century prize fighters to come in and train. These included three interesting boxers, Jem Mace, Thomas Sayers, and Bob Fitzsimmons.

Jem was declared Champion of England in 1861 and recorded his last fight in 1909 at the age of 78. Thomas started fighting in 1849, when there were no formal weight divisions. His last fight took two hours and ten minutes, was 42 rounds, and ended when the crowd invaded the ring. Police moved in to put a stop to proceedings eventually and the referee declared a draw. This was not even his longest fight. That was against Harry Paulson and was 3 hours and 8 minutes and 102 rounds – which he did win. Bob Fitzsimmons made boxing history as the sport's first three-division world champion – middleweight (1891), heavyweight (1896) and light heavyweight (1906).

Back to the referendum, the results were overwhelming in favour of yes, with just over 75% of the village voting for us to stay in the European Union. There isn't a breakdown for the 2016 referendum – Chipperfield is part of the Dacorum Local Authority and in that they just voted to leave by Leave: 50.67% to 49.33%.

My involvement in the Young Liberals started in earnest in 1975. Joining the local YL branch for Hemel Hempstead I tried to travel to my first Young Liberal Conference in April with our local Young Liberal chair in his Reliant Robin car. For those who don't know the Robin - it has only three wheels - which is fine on normal days, but that Easter in 1975 we had had a large blanket of snow. We managed one junction on the M1 motorway as every fifty or a hundred yards we would start to slide into the side of the motorway because the car's control was lost. My first Young Liberal conference would have to wait.

## Election Agent

If you were growing up in the mid-1970s there were stories about the hippie trail in the media - this romantic idea of traveling from London to Katmandu or Delhi or Manderley.

As the end of my time at Kings Langley school approached, I started to plan for an adventure. Rumour had it that Edward Kennedy might seek the US Presidency in 1976, and if he did I wanted to be part of the campaign. My plan was to travel overland from London through Europe and Asia to the US and to volunteer in California for the Kennedy campaign. I had been accepted to study Physics at Surrey University and I took a deferred entrance. This was something that many Universities liked their students to do, so that when they arrived they had experienced more of the world. As I travelled Kennedy made the announcement that he would not seek the Presidency so I was offered the chance to come back from Thailand and to work to re-elect the Liberal councillor for my village. Perhaps it wasn't going to be helping to elect the next president of the US but it would be fun.

I returned from my world travels having spent over six months travelling overland to Thailand via a 24-hour stopover in Moscow flying Aeroflot – a real experience in those days!! I started to work for Ian Senior, the Liberal Councillor for Chipperfield. The election would be on May 6th so I had the chance to cut my teeth working with him on my first real campaign.

Ian was a very good Councillor, working diligently for his constituents, and very popular. He had won the seat in a by-election (in the US it's called a special election) in what had always been a conservative area. We knew it would be difficult, but we threw ourselves into the campaigning and I loved knocking on doors and chatting to people in the village, many of whom knew me. We were looking to reduce the Labour vote as much as we could because the area would never return a Labour councillor. Chipperfield, like many of the small villages circulating London were full of stock brokers who were commuting to London. It turned out to be a close election, but one we lost by three votes with a 70% turnout – an amazing level for a local election.  I learned a lot from the election which I would use in future elections.

I was already spending some time in Saint Albans at the Liberal Club there, where not only the Saint Albans Young Liberals met but also the newly-founded Herefordshire Young Liberals, which I was to become Chair of. The Saint Albans YL group led by John Gunner was a lot of fun to hang out with. Gunner would for one year (1982-83) join the Young Liberal National Executive Committee, also he would be best man at my wedding, and would actually come on the honeymoon with Rosie and me. This is part of the speech to the Herefordshire Young Liberals Conference which secured my victory in the contest for chairmanship:

*"Good afternoon friends, this day may well be an important one in the Young Liberal movement in Hertfordshire. I truly hope it is. Some of you may be despondent at our poor showing in the local elections. Don't be. Today our dream of the Liberal Party taking off is greater than it was even in '74.*

*There will be elections held by Proportional Representation to the parliaments in Brussels and to Scotland. There is no way a British parliament can go without electoral reform (author I clearly was wrong here!)*
*We are a party of youth, of vision, of ideals and of aspirations to create a better world. What we need is liberal revolution."* (Dodds, 1976)

As you might imagine, my political activities impacted on my A-level results. I knew they would, and so in applying for universities I was looking for one which was offering me grades I thought I might get and which had a great atmosphere. I had at one time hoped to be an astronomer – like many of my generation, I was inspired by the space programme, the landing on the moon, and Star Trek *"to boldly go where no one has gone before"*. The reality was that there were few places to go to study astronomy and they expected very, very good grades. Something I wasn't going to achieve.

I had before I made that decision undertaken my work experience as a 16-year-old at the Bayfordbury Observatory. I loved the idea of working on the stars and had a telescope since I was eight. I also knew I had a new passion - politics - and the question was how best to enjoy that. When it came to applying to universities, I had applied to do Politics at Warwick University and also Physics at Warwick, Ecology at Lancaster, and Physics at Surrey. In the end, I decided to do Physics at Surrey for a couple of reasons – my physics teacher had gone there and said it was a great university, and when I visited it I really liked the mood and layout of the university. I also recognized that I had a real problem with grammar - but it wasn't until much later in life I found out I was dyslexic.

# Chapter 2
# Student Politics

*"I discovered that night (in his college's student politics) that an audience has a feel to it, and, in the parlance of the theater, that audience and I were together."* Ronald Reagan

Surrey University had been part of Harold Wilson's education reform started in the mid-1960s where Labour expanded comprehensive education (1965) to provide an entitlement curriculum to all children, without selection whether due to financial considerations or attainment. In the same time Labour expanded the number of universities. The government also wonderfully set up the Open University, to give adults who had missed out on tertiary education a second chance through part-time study and distance learning. Surrey University (1966) was one of the new Universities it had originally been Battersea Technical College. It also moved from inside London (Battersea Park) to the Surrey countryside around Guildford. The cathedral that overlooks the city and which the university is bumped up against was made famous by the 1976 horror movie "The Omen." It would also be where I would with other students receive my graduation certificate.

## Young Liberal Conference, Great Yarmouth (1976)

My first Young Liberal Conference was in April 1976 was over the Easter weekend, and I arrived there with many of the St Albans YLs. We brought tents and stayed outside the city at a campground. I have never liked camping, and so this was not fun, but the conference itself was. I stood for Galactic Emperor but didn't get elected. I think Pat Colman was elected. My hat, one I had brought back from Afghanistan it looked like a Davey Crocket hat - was very popular. We spent an evening in St Albans Liberal Club before going to the YL Conference trying to decide on the name of the hat. In the end we had named the hat Felix the other choice for a name was Dino….so I guess I am happy that it turned out to be Felix, otherwise I would have been doing this political work as Dino Dodds – which reminds me of Dean Martin, or the character out of the Flintstones Dino the pet Dinosaur.

## Liberal Assembly, Llandudno (1976)

My first party conference was in September 1976 in Llandudno on the coast of northern Wales, I realized that no one remembered my (given) name, and most attendees had decided that I was Felix. After a real attempt to correct people, I gave up. As the Conference dovetailed into my going to University, Felix became the name I was known by at Surrey University and forevermore. Earlier in the year I had supported John Pardoe in the leadership election against David Steel, as had many radicals. Steel had won with a large majority (12,541 to 7,032). I remember being part of a rebellion on the floor of the conference, but for the life of me can't remember what we were rebelling for or against. In retrospect, my opposition to David Steel was from the beginning of his tenure as party leader to the end of it in 1989.

*Figure 1: John Pardoe*

## University Liberal Club at Surrey University (1976-79)

Arriving at Surrey University after my travels and the Liberal Party Conference, I was ready to study again and very lucky to have some great lecturers in the Physics Department. As any new student would, I was definitely enjoying the first term …well the first year!!! I joined a number of clubs and was a DJ for the University Radio Station. I had the 9-11pm slot on a Saturday night called *"Transatlantic Express"* which played a bit of jazz and the music of *"love"*. I also had the chance to get involved in student politics.

When I arrived, there was no Liberal club. The University had an International Marxist Group (IMG) club, the Conservative club, and a weak Labour club. One of the first things I did was set up a Liberal club, and for the three years I was at Surrey it became one of the most effective, impactful and influential political clubs.

## Student Politics

I had arrived at Surrey University in October 1976, over a year after a famous election for President of the Students Union between Tom Poole, Steve Peace and Orlando the cat. It seemed very funny at the time because Orlando was a close second to Tom.

Surrey Students Union was one of the last student bodies not to be run by an Executive Committee. Instead it had two General Meetings (GMs) every week. These GMs could be attended by less than 100 to more than 2,000 on big issues, which for a University of only 3,000 was amazing. What this taught me was how to debate. The President, a sabbatical position, in my first year was Ian Ayers, who though a Liberal had been elected on a nonaligned ticket and governed from that. The Vice President the other sabbatical was Sheila Marsh who was a member of the International Marxist Group (IMG) but also a very effective Vice President focusing on student social and health issues.

Early on I was elected National Union of Students (NUS) Secretary, and stood to be a delegate at the 1977 NUS conference. I came third, which was an amazing achievement for a first-year student. I would of course like to say it was my liberal political platform, but I didn't run on that. I ran on a *"young, active and viral"* ticket …not my finest moment but it did get me to the Conference.

In national student politics, the Liberals were in a coalition called *"The Broad Left"* which also included Labour, Plaid Cymru (Welsh nationalists), the Communist Party and other non-aliened supports fighting against the Conservative and Trotskyist student groups.

During my time at University, all the NUS Presidents came from the Broad Left coalition. Charles Clarke (Labour) became a future Home Secretary in the Labour government of Tony Blair, and Sue Slipman (Communist), joined the Social Democratic Party of David Owen, where she said at their 1987 Conference:

*"The SDP should retain the classless opportunities provided by Thatcherism".* Indicating that the SDP would be a party of the right of centre.

Trevor Philips, (non-aligned) became chair of the Equality and Human Rights Commission (EHRC) and a television executive and presenter. And finally, the one person in the Broad Left coalition whom I have most positive memories of was David Aaronovitch (Communist), who became a formidable journalist. I was to get know David better in the coming months as university after university responded to the government's increase in tuition fees for self-financing students and overseas students by going into occupation.

**The occupation**
In March 1977, like students at other universities across the country, we at Surrey prepared to occupy university buildings over the tuition fees increase for overseas and self-financing students who had already committed to come to Surry. These fees would come in in September. I was elected to a seven-member Occupation Organization Committee and took responsibility to be a Press Officer for the occupation which had been endorsed nearly unanimously at a meeting of over 500 students. We then marched on the University Senate building where the University Senate was actually meeting about the same issue under its very able Vice Chancellor, Tony Kelly.

Anthony Kelly

A small group of us went into the Senate meeting room and informed those present very politely that we were now occupying the building and would not be leaving until the university refused to increase the fees for our fellow students. Some of the Senators were clearly unhappy. One called us *'fascist'*, but was calmed down by Professor Otto Pick.

Professor Pick was one of the stars of the university and a former advisor to Teddy Kennedy. He had been one of nearly 700 Jewish children in Prague who had escaped the Nazis with the help of a British diplomat named Nicholas Winton. Winton organized a total of eight locomotives to transport the children from certain death in Prague to London.

Professor Pick was someone you would miss your own lectures to listen to. He would talk about global politics as he had met and was friends with many of key political players.

Listening to him it seemed for those moments that you were observing global decision-making. During the occupation, he also led the support for the students among the Senators. We would meet with him regularly through the two weeks of the occupation.

*Figure 2: Professor Otto Pick*

The University Senate building was evacuated by its faculty and staff after the polite confrontation described above, and the students took control. We updated NUS about the state of the occupation, and NUS national officer David Aaronovitch was assigned to work with us on what needed to be done during the occupation. One of our concerns was to ensure that there were no reprisals to the leaders of the occupation by the University. He came down to the University twice during the occupation to show NUS support, and gave us excellent advice which was very much appreciated.

We had a Rota for students to sleep on the Senate floor, which we had also turned into an evening folk club venue. We also turned the Vice Chancellor's suite into the union coffee bar. Vice Chancellor Tony Kelly would come at the beginning of the day to get his coffee. This was one of his ways of showing his support for what the students were doing. He was a great VC.

Although we had gone in to occupation with nearly majority support of the students, there were clearly some students against the occupation. We decided to put the Greek students in charge of security both to ensure our safety and also to ensure no one took anything that didn't belong to them. I was very happy that we had done this because at the end of the first week the Rugby Club, having had some drinks, thought they would go over and stop the occupation. They never stood a chance! Oh, I may have forgotten to say the reason why we choose the Greek students. This is because they had come to the university after completing their national service and so had military training. When the Greeks met the Rugby Club students, there were a few bloody noses, but none of them belonged to students in the occupation. The Rugby Club never returned.

At the end of the first week, I was called to see the head of my department, a wonderful nuclear physicist, Professor Daphne Jackson. It was unusual to see a woman in that period heading a science department. She was clearly engaged at the forefront of her work. I was already a huge fan of hers both as a great lecturer and also because we were running a Union campaign to stop students going on their industrial year to South Africa. Professor Jackson made it clear that she would not support physics student doing their industrial year in South Africa. This was contrasted with the civil engineers, who seemed to have most of their students going there.

I of course knew what she wanted to see me about – the occupation and its impact on my studying. She made it absolutely clear that I had her total support and that there would be no repercussions due to me being away from lectures. She supported me a number of ways through my university career and would, when I graduated with only a pass degree, recommend me for a PHD in renewable technology at Strathcylde University. It was very tempting to imagine playing with windmills on the Orkney Islands. I have to also say that Prof Pick also tried to get me to do a Masters in International Relations at the University of Michigan, which he had strong contacts with. I was really appreciative of the support those professors gave me, but by then I was getting married and going traveling, so one door would close and another open.

After two weeks of its main offices being occupied by student protestors, the University made an offer of £50,000 UK pounds - which in today's value would be £220,000 for a hardship fund to help any overseas student in the coming year already studying to be able to continue his or her studies. Also, there was an agreement that there would be NO increase for on-going self-financing students. Another General Meeting was called. This time, nearly 1000 turned up, and we voted to end occupation, again nearly unanimously. Only one other university offered anything, and that was Bradford, which changed its collective mind when students left for the Easter break.

In 2008, Surrey University produced a history of its time from Battersea Technical College to present day and this is what they said about the events I have described:

*"This was also an unusually political period in campus life. In March 1977 students occupied part of Senate House for two weeks in protest at the Government's large and sudden increase in tuition fees, due to take effect the following autumn. Although most UK students were not affected (since their fees were paid by local authorities), self-financing students and overseas students were, and feelings ran high in universities throughout Britain. At Surrey, the University had already agreed to provide financial help during the first year of the increase, and the Vice-Chancellor wrote to the Prime Minister on behalf of Senate to protest at the increase."* (University of Surrey, 2008)

Vice Chancellor Tony Kelly was someone who supported the students in his time there and when I launched a student magazine in my final year called Insider, he did a column for us called Kelly's Eye.

**Young Liberal Conference Western Super Mare (1977)**

My last Young Conference for six years was in Western Super Mare, another nice holiday town.
The YL conferences are always held over the Easter period. The outgoing chair Steve Atack was handing over to Pat Coleman.

As I mentioned before I had been spending my Saturday evenings from 9-11pm as a radio DJ for Surrey University Radio Station. My show tried to have a short item on the news of the day it could be an interview or just our take on the issue of the day. I took the chance while at the YL Conference of interviewing Peter Hain who was then Honorary President of the Young Liberals. The interview was about his perspectives on the issues of the day and the rumour that he would leave the Liberals and join the Labour Party.

He would later that year defect to Labour with Simon Hebditch, another great thinker from the early 1970s. Simon would return to the Liberal fold in the late 1980s.

It turned out to be Neil Kinnock (future Labour Party leader) who persuaded him to join

Labour. At least the interview I gave where he claimed he had no intention of leaving the Liberal Party was broadcast before he did actually leave the party. In the interview, he denied he was leaving but would in fact do it for the Labour Conference in October 1977.

He and Simon explained his reasons in more depth in the booklet Radicals and Socialism published by the Institute for Workers Control. They said:

*"From the beginning, however, there was a major division in the radical Liberal camp between those (Mainly Young Liberals) who wanted a militant, confrontationist strategy, and those who believed that the priority was to get the Liberal party officially to adopt itself to the community politics idea, even at the cost of compromising on its militant and socialist basis."*

*"The Liberal Party has adopted a clear coalitionist strategy. The Origins of this were apparent in the 1973-74 period when the opinion polls showed that a substantial Liberal parliamentary representation was on the cards, and with it a situation in which the Party would hold the balance of power. Jeremy Thorpe (Liberal leader) came closer than many people realized to accepting a coalition offer from the defeated Edward Heath, and under David Steels leadership, the Liberals embarked on a strategy dependent upon obtaining the balance of pwer in successive hung parliaments, until one or other of the major Parties*

*is forced into formal coalition The Liberals also hope that the strategy will provoke a split in the Labour Party, with Labour's right hiving off to form a reconstituted 'socal democratic' party in the centre. Indeed, the basis of David Steel entered into the Lib-Lab Pack ws "to stop socialism". .... this strategy fits nearly into the modern Liberal approach of rational centrism, based on the belief that if everyone gets around the table and behaves like gentleman, then class divisions will melt away, industrial strife will end at a stroke and 'sanity' will prevail."* (Hain. 1978)

Rereading this it is amazing how accurate Hain and Hebditch turned out to be. It also explained the hostility that the party leadership would have to the Young Liberals of the 1980s when they thought they had gotten rid of the trouble makers.

The 1977 Conference had the feeling of the end of an era as we danced in the last night at a disco wearing our bellbottoms or flares.

The same year Peter continued his fight against fascism as he was one of the co-founders of the Anti-Nazi League (ANL). In the mid-1970s there had been an upturn in far-right wing group activities, some local election success and violence the National Front was even beating the Liberals in some parliamentary seats. I joined the ANL marches which often included a lot of music was an effective way to challenge the abhorrent views. I would go up to London for ANL marches through the East End where the National Front were gaining a hold.

Figure 3: Peter Hain's last speech to a Young Liberal Conference

**Deputy President**

Over the summer of 1977 the incumbent Deputy President of the Students Union failed his exams so I came back to University to the possibility of standing for that post. I did so and had broad support across political groupings because of the role I had played in the occupation.

In your second year, you were meant to live off campus. I was living around 7 miles away in a quaint town called Godalming (where WWF have their HQ), but being Deputy President, you had to be able to close the Union bar so you had to be on-site. This was one of the nice benefits which I may have expressed my fondness for a little too much. One of our students, Pete Brown, was a folk singer. He reworded parts of the song "Part of the Union" made famous by the Strawbs:

*"Now I'm a union man*

*Amazed at what I am*
*I say what I think, the company stinks*
*Yes, I'm a union man."* (Strawbs, 1973)

He converted the second verse to one about me becoming Deputy President just for a room on site. This was a tad embarrassing but a little true, too. I looked for the full lyrics he wrote but somewhere in my many moves I have lost them. Pete was such a great singer that we had him do concerts at Liberal Party Assemblies in future years.

The President this year taking over from a Liberal was a Conservative named Frank Downing. It wasn't easy for me to be his Deputy. It wasn't just our political differences, although they didn't help; it was the way he was running the Union. Our relationship got to a breaking point in the second term and I have to say it wasn't one of my best moments. We got him drunk one evening and took photos of him looking drunk –so people might question whether he should be our President. The main reason why we were looking to "no confidence" him was that a few weeks earlier he had tried to overturn the system of two General Meetings of students every week and replace it with an Executive Committee. We had succeeded in defeating that attempt overwhelmingly, with my summing up speech proving itself key to the vote.

*Figure 4: Frank Downing in the stocks*

We thought we had the support of the students for a no confidence vote on Frank – how wrong we were. They were not happy with the idea of the Executive Committee and had defeated it, but the idea of making a mockery of the President and trying to get rid of them did not go down well with them, and we were soundly defeated. This probably had a significant impact on the upcoming President elections for next year which I planned to stand in.

**Election for President**
I did stand at the end of my second year unsuccessfully for President of the Students Union. It was a strange election where the International Marxist Group proposed me, and the leading conservative proposed for the Labour candidate – there was no conservative candidate. I had the support from the last two Union Presidents Tom Poole (75/76 and Ian

Ayers (76/77). Perhaps Ian's supporting comments might have given me a clue of what was going to happen:

*"I would vote for Felix not because I think he would win, but because he is generally interested in the individual in me. Felix is one of the few whose interests are not to convert all to his way of thinking, he respects your different ideas and values them."* (Ayers, 1978)

My opponent Andy was a good candidate and ultimately a good President. He secured 776 (62%) votes to my 468 (38%). It was definitely a disappointment when I lost. I had stood on a ticket which included the Union buying property and setting up a Housing Association for renting out to students. There was a real possibility of converting a local warehouse into a block of flats. This could have helped us keep the housing costs down for students who were not on site. The students were not convinced. I felt I had done enough to be elected, and was also thinking ahead that I would then stand for National Union of Students (NUS)Executive the following year. This would help me gain a national base to engage in politics. NUS had been a place where many politicians started their careers. But the stupid no confidence motion against the sitting President that I had helped to engineer had backfired so much. My NUS political career was not to be.

# Chapter 3
# The Emergence of the *Green Guard*

*"Controlled and steady economic growth (in co-operation with our European partners), with greater attention to conservation of scarce resources, especially energy and land."*

Liberal Party Manifesto 1979

**The 1980's**

While Rosie, my wife, and I had been away in Egypt and Sudan on our honeymoon – for a year. British politics had gone through what seemed at the time a seismic change with the creation of the Social Democratic Party (SDP). The founding members or *"Gang of Four"* were Roy Jenkins (former Labour Deputy Leader), David Owen (former Labour Foreign Secretary), Bill Rodgers (former Labour Transport Secretary) and Shirley Williams (former Labour Education Minister). This *"Gang of Four"* should not to be confused with the Chinese Communist *Parties "Gang of Four"* who came to prominence during the Cultural Revolution (1966–76) and were later charged with a series of treasonous crimes. This gang's leading figure was Mao Zedong's last wife Jiang Qing. The other members were Zhang Chunqiao, Yao Wenyuan, and Wang Hongwenmet nor for that matter the post punk group the *"Gang of Four"*.

The SDP *"Gang of Four"* met at Dr Owen's house in Limehouse. They announced the new party and published the 'Limehouse Declaration,' which outlined their policies:

*"The progressive decay of the independence of the Labour Party, in the face of increased trade union involvement in all areas of Party policy and mechanism, has culminated in a catastrophic Wembley conference. As a result of this conference, the leadership of the Labour Party is now to be decided by a handful of trade union leaders in a smoke-filled room. This is the final straw for a Party which has been set on this course for the last twenty years. From the actions of the militant tendency, to the accusations of corruption from former Labour MPs such as Milne (1976) – it is now apparent that Labour is no longer a Party committed to parliamentary government.*

*In light of these changes, we propose in this document to begin a new force in the British polity. Ours will be a Council of Social Democracy – with a commitment to rally and represent all Britons who still hold the aforementioned principle of social democracy.*

*Ours will aim to create a society where no Briton will suffer discrimination based on issues of gender, race, religion, disability or sexuality."* (full text in Annex 1) (SDP, 1981)

Twenty-Eight Labour MPs and one Conservative MP joined and created the new Social Democratic Party (SDP). Many had been part of the Manifesto Group within the Labour Party, which was to the right, and had been battling the movement of Labour to the left. They positioned themselves between Labour and the Conservatives and decided in late 1981 to ally themselves with the Liberal Party in an "Alliance". This caused David Steel to announce to the Liberal Party faithful at the 1981 Party conference to:

*"Go back to your constituencies, and prepare for government!"* (Steel, 1981)

## Teaching

Now that I was back in the UK, it was time to look for a job. It seemed like a good idea to continue teaching because I had enjoyed it while in Khartoum.

Teaching was a lot of fun in Khartoum at the International School, I was teaching wide age groups from 8 to 18. The school had been set up a few years earlier and mostly had the children of Embassy staff, business and NGOs and high-level governmental officials. While at the school I did try and organize a trip to visit the Nubian pyramids but in the end the school wasn't sure they wanted such field trips which was a shame as I also never got to see those pyramids.

Every Wednesday afternoon I would have the 16-18-year-olds back to the flat for a discussion on current affairs. Ronald Reagan had been elected President of the United States and so there was much to talk about. It was a great chance to also see their insights about what was happening in Sudan. At this point in its history the President was Gaafar Muhammad an-Nimeiry who had taken power in a military coup in 1969 by what was called the Free Officers Movement. This was nine officers with Nimeiry at the centre. He initially focused on socialist policies with his party the Sudanese Socialist Union, but after several coups attempts by the communists (70,71,75,76) he moved closer to the US and away from Russia. In 1981, he was starting to move the country towards being an Islamic state thus alienating the predominantly Christian and animist south.

This contributed to with the finding of oil in the south and a nearly thirty years of civil war.

Over the years I kept in touch with one of my students, Ali Belail. His father was Elsheikh Hassan Belail, the Governor of the Bank of Sudan, who would die in jail after the successful coup against President Nimeiry by his Defence minister Gen. Abdel Rahman Swar al-Dahab.

At the subsequent election the pro-Islamist leader, Sadiq al-Mahdi, who had tried to oust Nimeiry in the 1976 coup, was elected. Mahdi was the great-grandson of Mohamed Ahmed Al-Mahdi, who had defeated Governor General Gordon and the British.

For many years I was addicted to Coca-Cola, and I definitely felt we needed some in the fridge in the flat in Khartoum. There was a problem to buy a new crate of Coca-Cola's, you had to give an empty crate. They wouldn't sell you a full crate. The question was where you got the empty crate from!!! It had been Ali's father who in the end had managed to get us an empty crate of Coca-Cola's. A very good example of the term Catch 22.

I'm sure the reader knows the term Catch 22 which joined the English language after the publishing of the book of the same title by Joseph Heller. Webster's defines Catch 22 as:

*"a problematic situation for which the only solution is denied by a circumstance inherent in the problem or by a rule."* (Webster, 2016).

Back to applying for jobs at schools in London. After a few interviews, I was offered a job to teach mathematics and physics at Harlington School near Heathrow Airport. As I had not done a teaching certificate I was put on a one-year probation and focused on becoming a good teacher. After six months living in rented property in Turnham Green we bought a house in Acton. We named the house Asgard I will come back to why later in the book.

We had chosen Acton to live because it was equidistant for Rosie to work at Kings College Hospital on nutrition and me to teach at Harlington School. Teaching mathematics and physics had not been my life plan, but it did give me lots of free time in the holidays to pursue politics.

Harlington was a split school with first (11-year olds) to third year (13-year olds) in an old school building close to one of the runways at Heathrow Airport. The 4th (14-year olds) to 6th Form (16-18-year olds) in another set of buildings two miles away. This could make it difficult to teach if you were teaching in old building up to the break and the other after the morning break you only had 15 minutes to switch campuses. Although those locations were only two miles away, we were only a few roads from Heathrow airport, so the roads did tend to be busy.

In time-bound tradition, a new teacher is an easy target for students, and so it was to be with me on a number of occasions. Those of you reading this who have taught will know it's the 13-year-old girls that often are the most difficult to teach. One incident that stands out was when I went into the maths walk-in storage closet to retrieve some books and they proceeded to lock me in for the rest of the lesson. There were a number of times in that first year when I was going home thinking I can't do this anymore. Somehow, I managed to survive the first year with the support of one of the other maths teachers, John Turner and my wife. Then in the second year miraculously the attitude softened, and it was as if I had survived my rights of passage. I really enjoyed teaching and tried my best while I was there to encourage the female students to succeed in mathematics and physics.

During my time at Harlington, I became the deputy representative for the more liberal teacher union, the National Association of Schoolmasters Union of Women's Teachers. This included helping to organize industrial action between 1984 and 1986 in support of a pay claim. I have always been a huge supporter of trade unions as a mechanism to support the rights of working people. The environmental movement and the trade unions have had a mixed relationship which is much better today but in the 1980s and 1990s. I often heard environmentalist's negative attitude towards trade unions because the unions seemed to be blocking the changes that environmentalists wanted.

I remember a discussion in 1997 in a bar after a meeting to prepare for the United Nations Conference Rio+5 with the Deputy Executive Director of the Environmental Investigation Agency (EIA). I hope it was the alcohol speaking, but he said if anyone tried to join a trade union at EIA he would show them the door. I have no idea if that was his personal view or

that of the organization, but he wasn't the only one who voiced opposition to trade unions. I worked with a number of people in the UK Trade Union Congress who tried to build bridges. people such as Deputy General Secretary David Lea and Paul Hachett (head of TUC Environmental Section).

While at Harlington I believe I tried to contribute fully to the school community. This included taking the children on school trips such as visiting the Centre for Alternative Technology (CAT) an eco-centre in Machynlleth in mid-Wales, dedicated to demonstrating and teaching sustainable development. This exposed the students to information on renewable energy, sustainable architecture, organic farming, gardening, and sustainable living. I also oversaw the chess club, working with a group of students on a school magazine and organizing a mock election around the 1987 General Election. In winter months a group of staff would enjoy Friday lunchtimes by going to the Great Western pub to play Trivial Pursuits – Baby Boomer version. I'm not sure if that would be allowed now.

With Facebook, I am still in contact with a couple of the students I taught in those years, and one of the teachers. Those were good times.

## Acton Young Liberals (1981-87)

In November, 1981 Rosie and I decided to go to a London Young Liberals meeting. The last YL meeting I had attended was a liberal student gathering at Imperial College in London in my last year at university (1979) with around 150+ people debating interesting topics. When Rosie and I arrived at Streatham Liberal Club three years later, it was shocking. I think there were around 20 people attending and debating a set of pathetic resolutions. That number included a couple of people who clearly were interested in shouting over you if they disagreed or snogging in the corner. There were some interesting people there and that was the first time I met Mike Harskin, Mike Cooper and Kieran Seale, who were clearly unhappy with the state of the youth wing.

Reading the 1981 *Young Liberal News* was really depressing. It said the highlight of the annual conference was: "the draw for the NLYL Grand Easter Draw. Retiring Chairman, John Leston made the draw at the Election Night Special Disco on the Sunday night. In the Miss World tradition, the last prize was drawn first." (Young Liberal News, 1981)

How the mighty had fallen! Could this really be the Young Liberals I had known in the mid-1970s?

*The Chairperson of the Young Liberals at the time was Sue Younger, and her perspective on the SDP was:*
*"It is the duty of the Young Liberals to make the Alliance a radical campaigning force and to stop its drift to the soggy centre."* (Younger, 1982)

This view fed my feeling that a strong (and more radical) voice was needed. In the spring of 1982 a group of us had started to develop a few ideas to try and bring some cohesion around the youth wing. The first was to launch a Young Liberal Philosophy group, and this was done with some other YLs who were unhappy at what was happening. They included Clive Buckman, Dylan Harris, Auriol Perry, Graem Peters and Kieran Seale. The leaflet started with a quote from Peter Hain from the famous 1971 Young Liberal publication the Scarborough Perspective:

*"Our philosophy evolves from a synthesis of radical thought. From socialism, we take our economic analysis, from anarchism our libertarian perspective, from syndicalism our commitment to workers control and from pacifism our commitment to non-violence."* (NLYL, 1971)

| |
|---|
| Some key Young Liberals in 1982-83 |
| *Kieran Seale:* Kieran focused on Ireland and economics. |
| *Dylan Harris:* Dylan tended to focus on constitutional issues. |

> *Clive Buckman:* Clive was part of the Greenwich branch with Dylan, Jo Nag and John Lamb. It and they would focus on issues of racism and peace.
> *Kathy Smith:* A very loud and aggressive Streatham YL who focused on gender issues.
> *Auriol Perry:* Auriol was one of the few intellectuals on the outgoing YL Executive team of 1982-1983. She was on the anarcho-syndicalist wing of the YLs, very bright and thoughtful. I think she had hoped for more intellectual discussions than in the end the YLs were capable of. She left the Party in 1984.
> *Graem Peters:* Graem was focused on the organizational aspects of the YLs and local politics. He was also an avid cricket fan

In 1982 I was paid for writing for the first time. I had through University been an avid reader of the *New Internationalist* and so submitted for their country profile section an article on Egypt.

For this I was paid the handsome fee of 25 UK pounds. The cheque was photocopied and framed and hung on my wall for a few years. I opened the country profile saying:

*"For centuries Egypt has evoked the world's imagination with ancient symbols of power and mystery: the pharaohs and the pyramid-builders, Tutankhamun, Cleopatra, the sphinx..."* (Dodds, 1982)

John Gummer, my best man at my wedding was now on the National League of Young Liberals (NLYL) National Executive (1982-1983) and we decided to work together on what would be my first article for *Young Liberal News*. It was called The British Response and dealt with the invasion of Lebanon by Israel. The Young Liberals working with others had persuaded the Middle East Councils of the three parties, Labour, Conservative and Liberal to jointly host a meeting in Central Hall Westminster under the title "Lebanon: A Human Tragedy". David Alton MP spoke at the event for the Liberals where he explained that the Party had passed a resolution (promoted by the YLS and Lord Mayhew) saying:

*"There can be no lasting peace in the Middle East (nor any genuine security for Israel) until the Palestinians' Right of Return to their homeland and the Palestinian right to self-determination are recognized."* (Dodds, 1982)

### Losing a Vote
Often people ask me how I got involved in green politics or environmental issues and my answer is that I lost a vote. This happened in the summer of 1982 when we called together in our new house Asgard a group of like-minded YLs, ex Liberal Students from Surrey,

and friends. My wife invited her sister Caroline who invited some of her friends that had been geography students at Leeds University.

In retrospect, this was the point when my life changed direction in relation to the main political focus I would have. The objective of the meeting was to agree what 'our' issue was going to be. All good political movements have an issue which brings them together and which gives them their first profile. I made a strong and passionate plea that it should be around social justice issues with an initial focus on being anti-apartheid and anti-Nazi.

I believed the YLs had a rich tradition in this area, having been at the forefront of the campaign to kick South Africa out of sports. My argument was that choosing this would enable the press to pick up on our actions quickly. We would be building on what had been achieved in the late 1960s and early 1970s by those YLs, because it already existed in the political and media zeitgeist.

At the meeting, others suggested ecology – green issues. When it came to the vote, the majority were for green issues, so our rallying call was to be on the environmental issues of the day. We had already established the Young Liberals Ecology Group under the leadership of Stephen Grey and Rosie Dodds. This would through the years produce some of our best campaign material on issues such as nuclear power and on acid rain. The YL Ecology Group also had its own quarterly magazine from 1982 to 1990. Stephen was at the age of 16 writing green speeches for Liberal MP David Alton. This was a good start to be a beacon for young concerned yoth interested in environmental issues.

### Direct Action
The YLs had a long tradition through the Red Guard era to take nonviolent direct action (NVDA), but by the beginning of the 1980s had forgotten how to do it.

After some preparation and workshops on NVDA, we decided on our first direct action. It would be in Croydon in south London at the Whitgift Shopping Centre. This is a shopping mall that has over 140 retailers under its iconic glass roof.

The Centre was in a Liberal Constituency having been won in the famous Croydon North West by-election the previous October when for the first time the SDP and the Liberals fielded a joint candidate. Bill Pitt looked very much like the media profile of a Liberal Party member at that time, because he was bearded and a little socially challenged.

Figure 5: Young Liberals preparing for Direct Action in Croydon

Back to the direct action. We planned to do some fly posting focused around the nuclear waste train that travelled through Croydon and the local campaign to have it re-routed around London. On a Saturday in late October 1982, arriving at what we thought was an early time 7am, which turned out to be a little late as many shops already had people going in to work, we quickly fly-posted a warning that the nuclear train had dropped its waste and people should evacuate. Unfortunately, the A3-size poster (11.69 x 16.53 inches) looked pathetically small on the windows of WH Smith. We had more success with leaving leaflets under car windows. The leaflets said that there had been a nuclear accident and that the car had been commandeered until the accident had been cleared up. This resulted in letters to the editor of the local paper over a number of weeks about the issue – no major papers covered it but it was a good start. I did feel a pang of guilt for the man

Figure 6: Felix Dodds at Daws Hill Peace Camp

who had left his car alone for a week because he believed the leaflet.

### Supreme NATO Headquarters Europe
In the autumn of 1982, High Wycombe Young Liberals were running a campaign against the building of a bunker to host the Supreme NATO Headquarters Europe in High Wycombe. The YLs already had a tent at what was called Daws Hill Peace Camp and a roster for people to come and stay; it was part of what was increasingly becoming a core set of issues we would campaign on over the next five years: Ecology, Peace and Northern Ireland.

A march was planned to the Supreme NATO Headquarters Europe on a cold mid-November evening. We met in High Wycombe Town Centre to hear a series of speeches.

Andy Binns, the Chair of the branch, came over and asked me to be the YL speaker. I had just rejoined the youth wing and there were YL National Executive Members there. But significantly there was also George Dunk who had been International Vice Chair during the mid-1970s. He remembered me and had seen what I was trying to do, and wanted to help, so he suggested to Andy that I speak. I was a little stage-struck, because there were over 5,000 people there and I hadn't spoken to that large an audience and was being asked to do it without any preparation. What also added to the stress was that I would be speaking after Lord Fenner Brockway.

Lord Brockway was a famous British antiwar activist. He had been arrested in 1915 as editor of the *Labour Leader* arguing against the British involvement in WW1. He was even held for one day in a dungeon in the Tower of London. He fought against imperialism and fascism supporting, active involved and recruiting for those fighting [Generalissimo Francisco] Franco in Spain. He won seats in the House of Commons a number of times, and when I met him, he was in the House of Lords. In 1951, he helped to found one of the UK's main development NGOs, "War on Want." There was also a statue of him in Red Lion Square. No pressure. I have no recollection of what I said, and then we were marching to the RAF Strike Command.

**This is Your Life**
This is Your Life is a famous TV programme produced sometimes on the BBC, but in the 1980s it was being produced by Thames Television for the 'other channel'. It was based on a US programme of the same name. In the 1980s the presenter was Eamonn Andrews and the concept of the show was very simple: the TV company without your knowledge would research your life working with friends and family and put together your life story that could be told in half an hour. Then the fun happened, where you were surprised by the host at a venue that friends or family had given them and exposed to the iconic statement:

*"xxxx, this is your life".*

In February 1983, Thames TV contacted me to ask if we could help with a programme they were doing for Jo Grimond, the former Liberal Party leader. Jo Grimond is rightly credited with rebuilding the Liberal Party and liberalism in the UK. He was the MP for Orkney and Shetland, the constituency (In the United States, an area, borough, or voting district) which is the farthest from Westminster and which I could see from my bedroom window in Thurso at the top of Scotland. He became leader the Liberal Party after the 1955 election, when the Liberal vote was just 2.5 percent. His principles and vision brought a new generation of people into the Party. He pitched the Party at the social liberal left of the Labour Party in keeping with the great Liberals of yesteryear, Lord Beveridge and John Maynard Keynes.

Figure 7: Rosie Dodds, Mike Cooper; Jane Godden and Paul Wiggin

*"Our long-term objective is clear: to replace the Labour Party as the progressive wing of politics in this country."* (Grimond, 1966)

We were more than happy to help Thames TV, but we wanted something in return, so we had the Thames TV props department make us 50 protest boards. I don't think we used them in the programme, but they were reused for many of our marches against apartheid, acid rain, nuclear weapons, nuclear power and any other demonstration we were on over the next few years. The Thames TV people definitely knew how to make those props!!!

The programme actually opened up at what was then the headquarters for TV-AM, which had launched only that week, and one of the people they were interviewing was Jo Grimond. The interviewer was none other than David Frost, who had gained worldwide fame for the Nixon interviews which he had completed in 1977. The first interview on Watergate drew 45 million viewers -- the largest television audience for a political interview in history, and a record that still stands. What many people don't know is that Frost funded the interviews himself and that Nixon got $600,000 plus 20 percent of any profit. After the shows, Gallup did a poll and it showed the 69 percent of the public thought Nixon was still trying to cover up, 72 percent thought he was guilty of obstructing justice and 75 percent that he should have no further role in public life.

Frost was also one of the famous five (at least in the UK) who fronted the new station TV-AM. The other four were also UK TV personalities Michael Parkinson, Angela Rippon, Anna Ford and Robert Kee.

As David and others brought Jo to the open plan, entrance area after the interview we Young Liberals were positioned by the ITV on the balcony which overlooked the entrance. Eamonn appeared from the shadows and walked up to Jo Grimond – who by now had a large smile on his face knowing what was about to be said: "Jo Grimond, This is Your Life!!!"

The cameras moved to the over 40 or so YLs (including my brother Simon) many wearing black and red berets, and some of us doing a raised fist salute and cheering for Jo. At this

time Simon had just moved in for a while to live with me and Rosie at Asgard (our house). The Young Liberals had decided that the berets would be part of our new image. We chose the clenched fist gesture because it could be traced back to the Spanish Civil War: this is where the Popular Front salute was once the standard salute of Republican forces. A letter from the Spanish Civil War states:

*"...the raised fist which greets you in Salud is not just a gesture—it means life and liberty being fought for and a greeting of solidarity with the democratic peoples of the world."* (Rolfe, 1937)

*Figure 8: Kathy Smith and Clive Buckman*

This is Your Life was not live TV, so now we had to be bussed back to the Thames TV studio where an audience was waiting. We followed Eamonn and Jo through the audience and up on to the stage. With Jo leading the way, we took up the back seats in what was a setting of a half-moon where you had perhaps four or five rows. Frost and Grimond would stand in the centre and the guest would walk through the centre of the half-moon seating. My brother also joined the event which was fun to have him along. The seats we were in were always used for the not so important people, but would fill the stage and were in all the shots.

*Figure 9: Graem Peters at Daws Hill Peace Camp*

With the help of Thames TV, we had given a clear message to the Party leadership there was trouble brewing in the YLs. To young people watching the show, our presence showed a vibrant radical youth wing. This was a time when many young political people had Che Guevara posters in their bedrooms. So, it showed YLs could be relevant and hip to them.

### Bermondsey by-election (February 1983)
Bermondsey was perhaps one of the most famous by-elections in British politics, at least in the last half of the twentieth century. This by-election was my first one. Let me explain why there was a by-election (what Americans call a "special election") in the first place: it was one of the aftermaths of the split up of the Labour Party. Some of the more right-wing

members had formed the SDP, while others just had had enough and wanted to get out of politics. The sitting Labour MP, Bob Mellish, just decided to leave his constituency had been infiltrated by far-left members and he was tired of fighting them. After his resignation, the local Labour Party chose Peter Tatchell, who was a contributor to *London Labour Briefing,* the magazine of the left, He had already caused waves because of an article he had written suggesting the use of extra-Parliamentary direct action by the Labour Party. This was of course exactly what the YLs were advocating and had been advocating through the *"Dual Approach"* to politics since the late 1960s. Which means:
"working both inside and outside the instruments of the political establishment" (Liberal Party, 1970)

Needless to say, this was not something the Liberal Party was happy with either.

Initially the Labour Party National Executive Committee met and narrowly rejected Tatchell as a candidate. This was challenged by the left wing of the Labour Party, which defended the right of Bermondsey to select its own candidate. Finally, this was agreed to, and Tatchell was duly selected again in January 1983. The right-wing press on a homophobic rant had already implied that Tatchell was gay. In those days, no sitting MP had said they were gay.

The Liberals had come second in the recent Greater London Elections (1981) for the constituency and they chose their Greater London Council (GLC) candidate, Simon Hughes, to fight the by-election. They thought this would give them a good chance as he was locally known and had already good support in the constituency. To add to the spice of the election the former right wing Labour leader of Southwark Borough Council, John O'Grady, decided to stand under the banner of the "Real Bermondsey Labour" with the former MP Bob Mellish's support and encouragement.

This was possibly one of the most vicious by-elections ever. The right-wing newspapers led by the Murdoch group (his papers included the Times, the Sunday Times, the Sun and the News of the World) helped by John O'Grady's campaign. They aggressively attached Peter Tatchell for being homosexual. O'Grady was even filmed touring the constituency on the back of a horse and cart, while singing a song which referred to Tatchell "wearing his trousers back to front".

The Labour Party constituency had been infiltrated by the hard-left Militant Tendency (Trotskyist group) as had others across the country, the most well-known being the Liverpool City Council, but I'll come back to that later.

Campaigning in Bermondsey was dangerous for your health – at the time of the by-election the constituency was very working class. We had not yet seen any of the development around the docklands or the selling off of council houses. There was huge intimidation by militants to try and ensure that Labour won this election. I remember campaigning in the Rockingham Estate – which now has a plaque to Peter Tatchell – when some of the people in flats there threw breeze brocks at us. It was not unusual for anyone who put up a Simon Hughes or other candidate poster in their window to have bricks thrown through it. Perhaps the song that expressed this time period best was The Tom Robinson Band's "Up Against the Wall":

*Dark-haired dangerous schoolkids*
*Vicious, suspicious sixteen*
*Jet-black blazers at the bus stop*
*Sullen, unhealthy and mean*
*Teenage guerillas on the tarmac*
*Fighting in the middle of the road*
*Supercharged FS1Es on the asphalt*
*The kids are coming in from the cold*

*Look out, listen can you hear it*
*Panic in the County Hall*
*Look out, listen can you hear it*
*Whitehall (got us) up against a wall*
*Up against the wall...*

*High wire fencing on the playground*
*High rise housing all around*
*High rise prices on the high street*
*High time to pull it all down*
*White boys kicking in a window*
*Straight girls watching where they gone*
*Never trust a copper in a crime car*
*Just whose side are you on?*

*Look out, listen can you hear it*
*Panic in the County Hall*
*Look out, listen can you hear it*
*Whitehall (got us) up against a wall*
*Up against the wall...*

*Consternation in Brixton*
*Rioting in Notting Hill Gate*
*Fascists marching on the high street*
*Carving up the welfare state*
*Operator get me the hotline*
*Father can you hear me at all?*
*Telephone kiosk out of order*
*Spraycan writing on the wall*

*Look out, listen can you hear it*
*Panic in the County Hall*
*Look out, listen can you hear it*
*Whitehall got us up against a wall*
*Up against the wall...* (Robinson, 1978)

This was a violent political time and the by-election seemed to be the epicentre of that violence for a few weeks. The Liberals were also playing into the anti-gay attacks on Tatchell, but from conflicting positions. Tatchell had already come out of the closet (as it was called in those days) but the Labour Party leadership had insisted he go back into the closet for the election. This angered some of the gay rights activists. The Liberal ones wore badges that said "I have been kissed by Peter Tatchell" or "I haven't been kissed by Peter Tatchell". The campaign team for Simon Hughes also produced the famous leaflet describing the contest as a "straight choice" between Liberal and Labour. Hughes was challenged on *Newsnight* about this 23 years later in 2006 when he was standing for the Liberal Democrat leadership. He admitted that it was "an unacceptable form of language", and said:

Figure 10: The Liberal 'This Election is A STRAUGHT CHOICE'

*"those are the sort of things that shouldn't have happened"* (Hughes, 2006).

He also acknowledged that the leaflet had acted as an inadvertent slur against Tatchell.

Simon Hughes won the seat with a whopping 50.9 percent swing, and retained the seat until the 2015 general election - 32 years later. The results:

| Liberal | Simon Hughes | 17,017 (57.7 per cent) | +50.9 per cent |
| Labour | Peter Tatchell | 7,698 (26.1 per cent) | −37.5 per cent |
| Real Bermondsey Labour | John O'Grady | 2,243 (7.6 per cent) | N/A |
| Conservative | Robert Hughes | 1,631 (5.5 per cent) | −19.4 per cent |

What a by-election to be involved with! Simon was to be an amazing MP for Bermondsey and was on the left of the Liberal and subsequently Liberal Democratic Party. He also became a friend.

While I was involved with the by-election my father decided to set up a management services company called Mainstay, and over the next four years, he would be engaged in helping a number of companies in their executive search. He also had the pleasure for a short time to be acting Director General of the British Museum as they helped find a full-time Director General. I know he enjoyed that time very much, not just for the challenge that the Museum was facing at the time but just the idea of running the Museum. He loved history, and now he had the chance to be around it while working...perfect!

## Young Liberal Conference Hastings (1983)

Going into the Hastings Conference in April 1983, outgoing national Chairperson Sue Younger confirmed the dire state of the youth wing in her outgoing editorial for YL News called "Fighting for Tomorrow" while trying to offer optimism:

*"We have pulled our organization back from what was undoubtedly the brink of extinction."* (Younger, 1983)

This was going to be the first outing for what was to become known as the "*Green Guard*" which took its name as a continuum from the late 1960s YLs who were known as the 'Red Guard'. *The "Red Guard"* had explored liberalism in its broadest terms, looking at libertarian socialist thinkers like Miguel Gimenez Igualada (1888-1973), Oscar Wilde (1854-1900) [also known as a successful playwriter], Rudolf Rocker (1873-1958) and Pierre-Joseph Proudhon (1809-1865) and anarchist thinkers like Michael Bakunin (1814-1876) and Peter Kropotkin (1842-1921). The *Green Guard* looked to Mahatma Gandhi (1869-1948), Robert Kennedy (1925-1968), Petra Kelly (1947-1992) and E. F. Schumacher (1911-1977) and an ideology that encompassed social justice, environment and grass roots democracy.

The *"Red Guard"* had been behind a lot of progressive policies that the Liberal Party adopted mostly against the wishes of Party leadership. The most important perhaps was the commitment to community politics and the dual approach to politics. It drew heavily from the United States Students for a Democratic Society (SDS) which was student activist movement which emerged in the 1960s as one of the main representations of the New Left. It was the youth branch of a socialist educational organization known as the League for Industrial Democracy (LID) Its political manifesto was the Port Huron Statement published in 1962 promoted a non-ideological call for participatory democracy it tried to balance the tension between communitarianism and individualism.

The Red Guard's equivalent to the Port Huron Statement was the Scarborough Perspectives (1971) which was a collection of essays:
- A New Perspective by Bernard Greaves
- Liberalism and Capitalism by Lawry Freedman
- Liberals in the Anarchist Camp by Simon Hebditch
- Community Politics by Gordon Lishman
- Democracy – and how to get there by Victor Anderson
- The Alternative Movement by Peter Hain

One of the key outcomes would be the successful advocating of the political strategy of community politics which was underpinned by the idea of participatory democracy. This was expressed through an Association of Liberal Councillors briefing as:

*"If the choice was between alternatives as stark as that, between conventional establishment politics or revolutionary confrontation, the outlook would be bleak indeed. But community politics offers a third choice of much greater flexibility and sophistication. We cannot say with any degree of certainty that it will succeed. What we can say is that it offers a real hope of bringing about a peaceful and accelerating transformation of politics depending upon the determination and skill with which it is applied.*

*That choice has been termed the 'dual approach'. It involves working simultaneously within and outside the established political system. The fusion of the two approaches creates a strategy distinctively, new and different when allied to the ideas of community politics.*

*We work through the established political structures not to win and exercise power but to remodel that structure itself; to create a new generation of political institutions corresponding to the reality of the pattern of communities that exist within society; to break down the centralised power structure of our society so that no single person or group possesses disproportionate power and all people and groups share the responsibility for controlling their own affairs.*

*To subvert and destroy the political establishment in such a radical way requires a powerful political movement based outside the political system. We work outside the political system, not to create confrontation or to foment revolution. It is indeed a more radical process than revolution."* (ALC, 1981)

Unfortunately, by 1983 community politics had in too many cases become more of an election machine to elect Liberal Councillors than what it had originally been expected to do. It had also on occasion tipped over into a kind of populist approach which could take up very illiberal positions, such as promoting a candidate as being a "straight fight" to insinuate that the opposing candidate was gay.

I was reading the July 2017 *Liberator* as I was writing this chapter and came across an article by one of the architects of community politics, Tony Greaves, who explains very well how he and others saw it:

*"Community politics as an expression and logical consequence of our Liberal ideology founded on free and autonomous people, working freely together in communities for the common good and bound together as citizens in our democracy."* (Greaves, 2017)

This reminds me of the William Gladstone (four-time Prime Minister of Great Britain.) quote about the difference between liberals and conservatives:

*"Liberalism is trust of the people tempered by prudence. Conservatism is distrust of the people tempered by fear."* (Gladstone, 1866)

At the April 1983 YL Conference, green-leaning candidates won a majority of the national executive seats as the conference also started to adopt green-facing politics. It wasn't that the YLs had not been interested before in green issues; in fact, they had supported the Liberal Party resolution of 1979 calling for a non-growth economic policy.

What happened in 1983 was the entrance of many 'green facing' members who were not yet working as a group – that cohesion would happen over the coming year. Members included: *Mike Harskin* (who died in 1992, but was then a Brent Councillor and editor of *Liberal News*), *Mike Cooper* (who became leader of Sutton Council), *Kieran Seale* (who became a member of the Liberal Democrat National Executive), *Pat O'Callaghan* (who would continue to fight on issues relating to Ireland), *Paul Wiggin* (who became a Peterborough Councillor and part of the rump Liberal Party that did not merge with the SDP), *Graem Peters* (who became a Bromley Councillor). They also had brought in more social justice-oriented members such as *Jatin Oza, Vijay Naidu and Jo Buckman*.

There were nine places on the National League of Young Liberals (NLYL) Executive for what they called National Members. I topped the National Member poll and was elected and also the poll to represent the Young Liberals on the Parties Council which met twice a year between National Liberal Party Conferences to agree new policy.

## UK Election (1983)

For the younger readers reading this book, it's important to remember that the Liberal/SDP Alliance had led in the opinion polls at the end of 1981 with a 16% margin over the rival Labour Party. As late as February 1982, before the drums of war for the conflict over the Falkland Islands started, the Liberal/SDP Alliance still had a six-point lead in the opinion polls.

Then came the ten-week war between Argentina and the UK for the Falkland Islands situated over 8000 miles away and positioned just off Argentina. The Islands represented some of the British Overseas Territories that were still under British rule. On the 2nd of April 1982, Argentina invaded and occupied the Falkland Islands, and the British government dispatched a naval task force to take on the Argentine Navy and Air Force. It then went on to retake the islands. The war was relatively short at 74 days' duration, and it ended with the Argentine surrender on 14 June 1982. The death toll was 649 Argentine military personnel, 255 British military personnel, and three Falkland Islanders. After the war the Conservatives had a 26% lead (51% Conservative, Labour 25%, Liberal/SDP 25%).

For every election, the National Executive of the Young Liberals put up a list of target seats that it suggested YLs should go and campaign in. The 1993 election itself had seen only three (out of nine) of the Young Liberal target seats return MPs. These seats were in Leeds West (**Michael Meadowcroft**), Liverpool Mossley Hill (**David Alton**) and Colne Valley (**Richard Wainwright**). The six who lost were in Croydon North West (Bill Pitt), Bow and Popular (Eric Flounders), Southport (Ian Brodie), Brown Harrow East (Dick Hains) and Pendle (Gordon Lishman).

Mike Harskin had been elected Publicity Vice Chair of the YLs and was probably the first for many years who actually was a journalist. He was a political genius and a great writer. For the 1983 June 9th election under his direction the YLs had produced a number of leaflets on:

- *Education: calling for more funding for education, more relevant education, and phasing out of exams;*
- *Unemployment: advocating a minimum wage of 110 UK pounds per week, and statutory safeguards for part-time employees to start making major reductions in the length of the working week;*

- *Women: supporting women's right to choose whether to have an abortion, and calling for women's health centres run by women, as well as more rape care centres and training for police on how to work with rape victims;*
- *Racism: calling for the disbanding of The Special Policy Group and all similarly destructive forms of policing to be disbanded, together with independent inspection of police files and independent research into and supervision of methods of integration;*
- *Environment: calling for more accountability for big business, protection of the rain forests, energy conservation, and increased funding of renewables;*
- *Sexual politics: calling for an end to discrimination against women and gays in employment and housing, and legal recognition of homosexual rape and rape within marriage;*
- *Northern Ireland: calling for HMG to fix a date for withdrawal of troops from Northern Ireland, a ban on rubber and plastic bullets, and the repeal of repressive legislation such as the Prevention of Terrorism Act and the Emergency Powers Act;*
- *Third world: calling for the cancellation of all previous debts, an increase Overseas Development Assistance (ODA) to 1 per cent of Gross National Product (GNP), guaranteed markets at a fair and stable price for goods.* (NLYL, 1983)

These leaflets helped YL branches recruit as many new members as possible. General elections for a youth wing are a great chance to have young people look at politics. For those that did, it was important to have something which might resonate with them available to entice them in. The leaflets were also bounded together into what we called 'an Alternative Manifesto, to the Liberal/SDP Alliance Manifesto – the press release that accompanied them started with the statement:

*"Young people would do just as well at home on June 9 if they go by the Alliance Manifesto." It went on to say: "We reject the capitalist view that everyone with enough money can make choices about their lives, but anyone without money is told what to do. We would say that no one should live in poverty and no one should earn too much."* (NLYL, 1983)

It was a direct appeal to left leaning greens, socialists and liberals. Some of the media response was supportive:

*"Young Liberals say that the violence in Northern Ireland will continue so long as Britain is there to provide one side with a permanent veto and to reinforce the bigotry of people such as Ian Paisley" The Irish Times*

*"The Young Liberals in their manifesto acknowledged deviations from the policies of their parent Party. They urge unilateral disarmament, withdrawal from NATO, a guaranteed minimum weekly wage for workers and the unemployed, a big increase in aid to the Third World, and closer political control over the police"* The Guardian

*"The Young Liberals reject the defence section of the Alliance manifesto and want to see Britain abandon nuclear weapons and NATO membership."* The Daily Mirror

*"Young Liberals believe in fighting racism from every angle. We are constantly tackling the myths about immigration. The Liberal Party and the YLs have a record of fighting for the rights of minorities that are second to none."* West Indian World (UK newspaper)

David Steel, on the other hand, was not happy. The Liberal leader's response was:

*"It will be just as well; if the Young Liberals stay home."*

As David Alton MP said when Mike died in 1992:

*"During the 1983 General Election, Mike Harskin ruffled more than a few feathers when, along with other Young Liberals, he issued an alternative Manifesto. It said quite a lot for his talent, skills and winning ways that over the following decade he carved out such a place for himself within the leadership of the Party, although mercifully never falling foul or sycophancy or a craving to be part of the establishment."* (Alton, 1992)

As I stood outside the press conference the Party was holding at the National Liberal Club in London handing out the Young Liberal press release, I asked Mike if he thought it was a good idea to hand it out. He just smiled and so I shrugged my shoulders, and with Mike handing our press release to the journalists, I thought, "Well this is just the beginning". Battle lines were being drawn between the Party leadership and the youth wing. Those lines would only get more vivid over the next few years as the Party leadership tried to move the Party to centre and the youth wing tried to move it to the left.

One of the amusing events during the General Election was when Mike decided that he wanted to get a Mrs. Thatcher (the Prime Minister) poster from Finchley, her constituency. Graeme, Mike and I piled into my car late one night and went over to see if we could pick one up. It was not our finest moment. Mike tried a number of houses, trying to pull Thatcher posters up from the gardens and failing until at one house he succeeded, and then a large dog started barking furiously. I started to drive away slowly with the door open as Mike was running after us with a broken 'Thatcher for Finchley' poster board.

Not happy with the damaged one he had, Mike decided to write to her after the election.

*Dear Mrs. Thatcher,*
*As a great admirer of yours, I wonder if you would be kind enough to send me a signed photograph of yourself?*
*May I be particularly bold and request one of your Finchley election posters from June (though I assume that they all went up in windows!)*
*Yours faithfully,*
Michael Harskin

He received a letter a week later from Number 10 from one of Mrs. Thatcher's Advisors.

*Dear Mr. Harskin,*
*The Prime Minister has asked me to thank you for your letter of 8 March, and to send you the enclosed signed photograph with her best wishes.*

*With regard to the Finchley election posters, I am sorry I must disappoint you. As you rightly anticipate, they have all been used.*
*Yours sincerely,*
Caroline Ryder

Mike would have to wait until the 1987 election before he got his poster, which he then showed off with pride on one of the walls of his room.

We did go out for a flyposting during the election with YL posters of a clenched fist and a slogan *"Power to the People"* - Vote Liberal. Deciding to fly post Covent Garden in Central London around 2:00 am our first stop would be a store opposite the tube station for the greatest impact. There were four of us in the car (me, my brother Simon, plus Kieran, and Mike). I think my brother had his Palestinian scarf on, and he was out of the car and busy putting the poster up. Mike and Kieran were arguing about something and so not keeping an eye open for the police. Before I knew it, the police had parked behind me and a nice City of London police

*Figure 11: Pat O'Callaghan International Vice Chair NLYL*

officer was knocking at my window. Simon was still putting the posters up, oblivious to the arrival of the police. I wound down my window and this very polite policeman said:

*"Hmm...Liberal flyposting; we don't see much of that. You know it's illegal."*

I nodded, by which time Simon had seen the police and stopped his fly posting and was looking more than a little guilty. The policeman said:

*"Look, we are just about to go off duty, and can't be bothered with the paperwork this would cause as this is not in our jurisdiction."*

They were City of London police and we were in the Metropolitan police district.

*"We are going to ask you to take the posters down and to go home with a warning."*

We all just nodded and got out to help Simon take the posters down. When we had finished, the officers got back into their car and waited for us to leave.

In UK politics, there have been a few radical Prime Ministers both from the left and the right. Most of the time the parties govern from the centre whether they were Labour or Conservative. There is no doubt that Mrs. Thatcher was a radical from the right exposing right wing economic liberal views. Her policies did great damage to the UK and started the move to greater inequality that we are seeing so clearly now, but she also showed that radicals could change the world. What we wanted in the YLs was Party leader that understood that and acted on it. Instead, we had David Steel. We wanted a "social liberal" alternative not a "social democratic" alternative.

In my article in the July *Young Liberal News* after the election, I tried to capture the vision we were putting forward of a different type of politics:

*"We as Young Liberals have argued for as long as I can remember that what is needed in this country is not government of the centre but of the radical left......This is a time when we must not retreat from the current crisis in this country by offering centrism but we must call for fundamental change. What we ask for – no 'demand is the Party campaign for a self-managed society which would be under people control and cooperative ownership. Liverpool Council is already doing this in Housing under the Chairmanship of Liberal Chris Davies. But we must go further by incorporating the philosophy of the environment which is characterized by the decentralization of the systems of production, economy and resource use in a way which will break up of the centralized corporations."* (Dodds, 1983)

In another article in the same newsletter looking at racism in the UK, Jatin Oza expressed the challenge that the UK would be facing based on its past.

*"As the Empire expanded with the continued use of force and brutality, the only way that a tiny country like Britain could hold vast areas in subjugation was to create an ideology whereby the subject people would accept and intensify their own subjugation. It was once the duty of the white man to bring Christianity to the world. Now it was their mission to bring civilization – civilization which made the colored people believe that to be white was to be superior."* (Oza, 1983)

## Meeting with Gerry Adams

The YLs had a strong policy on Northern Ireland and it was something I supported having lived there and experienced the discrimination. I lived in Newtownards in Northern Ireland in 1966-1967, when Northern Ireland was still split on religious grounds. James Craig, the first Northern Ireland Prime Minister, said in 1934:

*"All I boast of is that we are a Protestant Parliament and a Protestant State."*

The civil rights movement had already started up in Northern Ireland in 1964 and it was challenging what most other people in the UK did not even know was going on. If you lived in Northern Ireland:

- There was job discrimination – you had to say what religion you were when applying for a job so Catholics were less likely to be given certain jobs, especially government jobs;
- We didn't have one man, one vote – in Northern Ireland, only householders could vote in local elections, in the rest of the UK all adults could vote;
- There was gerrymandering of electoral boundaries – this ensured that Catholics who lived in particular areas had less voting power than unionists often even where Catholics were a majority
- The police force (Royal Ulster Constabulary or RUC) – was almost 100% Protestant and accused of sectarianism and police brutality
- Police were allowed to search without a warrant, arrest and imprison people without charge or trial, and could ban any assemblies or parades, and any publications.

In 1966 schools were also segregated. To explain my situation a little my mother was Protestant and my father Catholic and for my father's mother to agree to allow them to get married then the first born had to be baptized a Catholic. So, I was Catholic! I would be expected to go to the Catholic school, but because Rolls Royce was bringing a lot of jobs to NI, my father had some pull. I remember going to the Regent House Headmasters office with my parents as a ten-year-old. Regents House was one of the best 'protestant' schools in Northern Ireland. I was told I was NEVER to say I was Catholic.

For this book, I looked up the figures relating to the state of segregation in the Northern Ireland schools. Regents House was still vastly protestant – 75% (2012). The breakdown in Northern Ireland of school population is 51% Protestant, 37% Catholics and 12% others (all 2012).

*"Almost half of Northern Ireland's schoolchildren are being taught in schools where 95% or more of the pupils are of the same religion."* (Torney, 2012)

What many people perhaps do not know is that the Anglo-Irish Treaty of 1922 creating the Irish Free State did actually create it such that the expectation was it would eventually cover the whole of Ireland. Unfortunately, at the insistence of the northern protestant landowners, they had also inserted Article 12, which allowed for six counties in Northern Ireland to opt out of the Irish Free State. This is what they did the day after the act was passed by the British parliament. For nearly two days, Ireland was one state and then the politicians of Northern Ireland asked to rejoin the United Kingdom.

I was mostly oblivious to the sectarian divide in Ireland that was to explode shortly after we left for England in the summer of 1967. Unlike the rest of the UK the vote in Northern Ireland was based on you owning property. The general vote was confined to the occupier of a house and his wife. Occupiers' children over 21 and any servants were excluded from voting. There were also multiple votes held by business owners - known as the "business vote" and gerrymandering to establish a political advantage for the Protestants by manipulating district boundaries.

In August 1968, there was the first civil rights march, and August 1969 saw the first riots and the return to civil war in the UK. This included what is known as the Battle of Bogside 12-15th of August when violence broke out during the loyalist Apprentice Boys of Derry parade. It is seen as the first confrontation in what became known as *'the Troubles'*. On the 14th of August James Chichester-Clark the Prime Minister of Northern Ireland took the unprecedented step of requesting the Harold Wilson the British Labour Prime Minister for troops to be sent to Derry. He sent in a company of the 1st Battalion, Prince of Wales's Own Regiment of Yorkshire. Over 1000 people were injured during the rioting.

*The Troubles* would continue for nearly thirty years with 3532 deaths of which 60% were republicans and 30% loyalists and 10% British security forces. In addition, it is estimated that 107,000 were injured in the dispute.

Finally, it ended with the Good Friday Agreement of 1998 and the final decommissioning of the IRA weapons in September 2005. The agreement acknowledged:

Figure 12: Mike Hamill

- that the majority of the people of Northern Ireland wished to remain a part of the United Kingdom;
- that a substantial section of the people of Northern Ireland, and the majority of the people of the island of Ireland, wished to bring about a united Ireland.

Back to 1983 when Gerry Adams was elected for Sinn Fein for the first time to the House of Commons for Belfast West. He was re-elected in 1987 and then again in 1997 to 2011. He never took up his seat in parliament as he saw it as a foreign occupying parliament.

An interesting fact that people may find hard to believe is that the two major soccer teams in Scotland were based on religion – Celtics were Catholic and Rangers Protestant. It was only in 1989 that Rangers signed their first major Roman Catholic player "Mo" Johnson.

In the summer of 1983, I and some other YLs (Kieran Seale, Pat O'Callaghan, Mike Hamill, Janice Turner and Mike Harskin) met with Gerry Adams to ask him to take his seat in parliament and to argue his cause there. Also, with us was Ken Livingstone, the Labour Mayor of London, and the future leader of the Labour Party, Jeremy Corbyn. If you had asked me then which of these two would become leader of the Labour Party I would have with a 100% certainty said Ken.

We also discussed where we could work with Sinn Fein on issues like Troops Out, and at the same time we denounced the use of violence. We were, not surprisingly, condemned by the David Steel for what he termed 'bringing the Party into disrepute'.

*"At one point, it was reported that a Sinn Fein supporter moving to England asked Gerry Adams which British political Party he should work with, and was told to join the Young Liberals."* (Harskin, 1988)

The first Young Liberal Council after the election in August 1983 was controversial because there were some who wanted to put forward a no-confidence resolution in Mike Harskin. Mike, in his usual media savvy way, and always one step ahead of his detractors, had let some of the journalists know that Gerry Adams might turn up. I can't remember if we ever invited him, but it did add to the fun of the Council with everyone wondering whether he would or would not turn up.

With Mike an Officer on the YL Executive Committee, it seemed most obvious that he should be the candidate of the group for Chairperson in the 1984 election. He and I discussed it, and I suggested that he stand for election. He, on the other hand, wanted me to stand for the position, because he saw me as more of a uniting figure and himself as more of a divisive figure within the YLs. I'm not sure I agreed with that characterization, but after consulting others and Rosie I decided that I would challenge the sitting Chairperson, Janice Turner, in April 1984. Now the challenge was that we had to put together a campaign team capable of defeating an incumbent, something that is never easy.

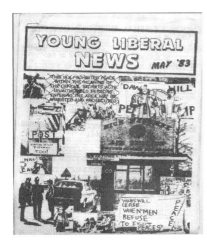

## Young Liberal News

Where ever I have worked I have recognized the power of the media and have tried to ensure I have some role in using it to frame the political narrative. At university this was through the magazine I set up *Insider,* while I was Executive Director of Stakeholder Forum and working around the UN it was through our daily newsletter *Outreach* and in the Young Liberals it was primarily through *Young Liberal News*.

The impact that *Young Liberal News* had in creating a vision and message from 1983 to 1987 cannot be overestimated. Mike Cooper took over the YL News editorial board, and with Mike Harskin, then Publicity

Vice Chair, revolutionized *Young Liberal News* in design and in making it especially known for provocative covers.

The May 1983 issue had a collage of photos of Young Liberals at Daws Hill Peace Camp, including confronting police there. One of the signs at the peace camp was for where the mail could be delivered had under the name POST (which had a peace sign in the O) a placard saying "Cruse Kills Postman TOO!" Peace and anti-nuclear pages became staples of the front cover over the next four years.

The July 1983 issue had photos of Tony Benn and Ken Livingston on the front cover under the heading, "Tony and Ken the natural leaders".

The YL News Feb-March 1984 issue front cover was the Kremlin Ward By-Election: Sensational Win! Chernenko Victory under photo of Chernenko. This was followed by Chegwyn (Peter Chegwyn was one of the key architects of Liberal by-election victories) sought by KGB…Steel claims: "Great Alliance Victory" Kremlin Backs Fair Votes Campaign.

By November 1983 the pitch for the new vision of the YLs was becoming clearer. The YL News Editorial said, *"Think globally, act locally is becoming the catchphrase of the* 'new politics."

The editorial also started to draw the lines between the current Chairperson Janice Turner and the new wave of YLs. It continued by saying

*"Lots of YLs kid themselves they are thinking on a global scale just by concentrating on international affairs. This is badly misinterpreting the philosophy. What they are doing is thinking locally: on one issue. Globally means all humanity – not just the trendy liberation struggles in exotic sounding parts of the world."* (YL News, 1983)

Again, provocative language could be found in the newsletters with headings such as *'Bolsheviks in Blackpool'* attacking the Conservative Conference held there. I also wrote an article in preparation for the 1984 philosophy commission:

*"Our industrial policy bears much resemblance to the 20th century Anarcho-Syndicalism (i.e. workers control). It rejects Trade Unions and Management system as this creates a*

*conflict situation. It also allows us to reject the class basis of society and develop a classless one which Liberals believe in. Jo Grimond whilst Liberal leader in the sixties flirted with Anarcho-Syndicalism."* (Dodds, 1983)

As reported in *Young Liberal News*, the Liberal Party Council on November 26th in Darlington saw Pat O'Callaghan (YL International Vice Chair) successfully steered another Northern Ireland motion through Council – calling for a return to normal judicial procedures in the six counties and criticizing the use of supergrasses.

In the British criminal world, police informants have been called "grasses" since the late 1930s, and the "super" prefix was coined by journalists in the early 1970s to describe those who witnessed against fellow criminals in a series of high-profile mass trials at the time.

Not to be confused by the English rock band Supergrass which won New Musical Express (NME) Best New Band in 1995.

The Liberal Party also at its Council meeting in November 1983 passed a motion by a substantive majority calling for the cancelling of the deployment of Cruise missiles in Britain.

Another motion reaffirmed the Liberal Party's commitment to full equality for homosexual and heterosexual men and women, their protection against discrimination on the grounds of sexuality and the introduction of a Bill of Rights with specific guarantees for homosexuals. (YL News, 1983)

The Christmas issue (1983) had a mock Christmas message for the YLs from David Steel, which was funny if looked at in light of what the YLs had done in the general election:

*"This being a festive season, it is my pleasure to thank you for your efforts in the past year to promote Liberalism – especially in campaigning during the election. I strongly recommend to you all the idea of a brief 'sabbatical', if you get the chance over the Christmas period,"* Steel wrote.

The Christmas issue also continued the ongoing look at different political philosophies, and this time I worked with Mike Harskin on the article on Social Democracy:

*"In the post-war period, Social Democracy became associated with adaptability, mild reformism, but with the undertones of centralism and bureaucracy. ...It is best recognized as a way of running a structure...or efficient management."* (Dodds 1983)

The January 1987 issue had police on horses attacking a young woman. The photo was taken either in the Miners dispute or the demonstration against Rupert Murdoch in Wapping as part of the dispute between him and the National Union of Journalists.

My favourite was one for the 1986 Liberal Party Assembly which has workers breaking through the floor into a dining room with many rich overlords having their dinner.

The Young Liberal policy on the media passed at the November 1983 Stevenage Young Liberal Council said "We believe a Liberal society requires a free and open press, that is owned and controlled by the communities it serves."

### Chesterfield by-election March 1984

The Chesterfield by-election, was held on 1 March 1984 following the resignation of the sitting Labour Member of Parliament (MP) Eric Varley. The Liberals put up a local candidate named Max Payne, who was a philosophy lecturer at Sheffield University. The Party leadership wanted to replace Max, who was far from an ideal candidate. Some people called him arrogant and difficult to work with, the Party leadership was also uneasy because Labour had chosen Tony Benn, a former Minister and intellectual powerhouse of the what most people perceived as the hard left. But Payne was not for turning – to paraphrase a famous saying from Mrs. Thatcher, the Prime Minister of the time.

In 1981, Benn had challenged Denis Healey for the deputy leadership of the Labour Party and came very close to winning (50.4% Healey to 49.6% for Benn). This had precipitated the creation of the Social Democratic Party and his opponent at the time was reported to have said afterwards that had Benn won, he would have destroyed Labour as a force in twentieth-century British politics. Benn had lost his Bristol South east seat in the 1983 general election.

As was the case for many by-elections, the Liberals had put together a great team to run the campaign. The election agent was the guru of by-election wins Peter Chegwyn, and also in his team was Young Liberal Olly Grender. The YLs from London organized a bus up to campaign over one of the weekends of the by-election. The Liberal campaign team believed because of the rhetoric of the new YLs that we were coming up to campaign for Tony Benn. I have to admit that this might have been spurred on by a front page of *Young*

*Liberal News* after the 1983 general election. It had as I have said a photo of Tony Benn and Ken Livingstone and the heading "Our Natural Leaders". I can't remember if this was Mike Harskin's doing or the newsletter editor Mike Cooper, or them both having fun. The result was near panic when we arrived at the Liberal HQ in Chesterfield.

Although we had many seasoned by-election YLs ready to canvas, they decided they couldn't afford to let us canvass as we might be either telling people to vote for Benn or filling in the returns wrong on purpose. So, we found ourselves delivering leaflets – a big waste considering our talents, but at this point we didn't realize they thought we had come up to support Benn. Mike borrowed my Walkman, and got so into the music that he ended up delivering half the leaflets in the wrong constituency.

The eventual winner was Tony Benn. He defeated sixteen other candidates, which at the time was the largest field in a British by-election.

| Labour | Tony Benn | 24,633 | (46.5 percent) | -1.6 percent |
| Liberal | Max Payne | 18,369 | (34.7 percent) | +15.1 percent |
| Conservative | Nick Bourne | 8,028 | (15.2 percent) | -17.0 percent |

This wasn't the first controversial by-election that Chesterfield had had. There was another in 1913 a time of a Liberal government and a growing Labour Party. The sitting MP had been elected as a Liberal MP but had been sponsored by the Miners' Federation of Great Britain and the Derbyshire Miners' Association. When he took office, the Miner's Federation became affiliated with the Labour Party, and they told all MPs they had supported to join the Labour Party, which James Haslam did. He died in 1913 causing the by election, and then the question was would the Liberals and Labour contest it or find a compromise. The Derbyshire miners had selected Barnet Kenyon to be the Labour candidate and the Liberal Association George Eastwood, the President of Chesterfield Division. The Liberals seeking a compromise stood down their candidate but did not formally adopt Kenyon and decided to rely on his nomination as the Miners' candidate in the expectation he would take the Liberal whip once elected to Parliament. This he did, and in return he would be known as the Labour-Progressive member and would have full freedom to speak and vote as he wished on issues affecting mining and labour. But this compromise between the two parties fell apart with the national Labour Party putting up a candidate of their own two days before closure of nominations. Labour leader Ramsey MacDonald told the Mining Federation that candidates like Kenyon were damaging the Labour Party nationally and compromising its existence as an independent Party. The seat was then reported as a gain from Labour to Liberals and the switch also had an interesting impact where three former mining constituency Liberal MPs that had switched to Labour retook the Liberal whip.

When Tony Benn stood down as the MP for Chesterfield the Liberal Democrats won the seat in the 2001 election having been second in the elections since the by-election in 1984. They would hold the seat until the 2010 election losing a close fought challenge with the seat returning to Labour.

**Young Liberal Conference Torbay (April 1984)**
The 1984 YL Conference in Torbay had two Commissions: one on Philosophy, and the other on Criminal Justice. For the Philosophy Commission we produced "Six Essays in Search of a Philosophy" with contributions from Auriol Perry, Neil Schofield, Dylan Harris, Andy Binns, Derek Jackson, Mike Harskin and Felix Dodds.

The introduction was by Lord Tim Beaumont who would leave the party in 1999 to join the Green Party but in 1984 in the introduction he echoed much of the thoughts of the Young Liberals when he said:

*"As we become a bigger Party we will become in some ways less radical in our policies, because Radicals are always in a minority in parliament in Britain. We are seeing this already with the Alliance. But this will not matter if we remain radical in our philosophy and in the structure, which stem from that philosophy. Policies are bound to change but if we have helped give back 'power to the people' we will have accomplished a lasting revolution.*

*It was given to my generation, which was brought up on that great book 'The Strange Death of Liberal England', to help conceive a new Liberal revival. It is the duty of this general to prepare for 'The Strange Birth of Liberal Britain'.*

*Conception is more fun than birth but they are both necessary and the later is more rewarding! I congratulate and envy the Young Liberals in their task."* (Beaumont, 1984)

Former Liberal MP Bill Pitt and incoming honorary President of the Young Liberals Des Wilson were among the guest speakers at that conference.

In the Conference issue of *Young Liberal News,* leading YLs criticized the new Liberal/Social Democrat Party (SDP) Commission on Northern Ireland. Mike Hamill from the YLs, also a counselor in Harrow, said:

*"He (Steel) is just packing it with his friends who will come up with a 'sensible policy' from his point of view. Five of the seven Liberal members on the Commission are known to hold pro-Unionist views." Hamill went on to say: "It is an attempt to change the policy by the back door ...[the commission] will prepare a long document and submit it to Party*

*assembly. But it will be presented in such a way that if you vote against it, you will be voting against the Alliance."* (Hamill, 1984)

In another article in *Young Liberal News,* Pat O'Callaghan argued:

*"In August 1979, British troops first went onto the streets of Northern Ireland...After 5 years the goals or peace and stability seem further away, and it has become clear that British troops are part of the problem not part of the solution."* (O'Callaghan, 1984)

The April Conference issue also saw David Steel, the Party leader, sit down for an interview with the two people he probably most wished would leave the YLs, Mike Harskin and me.

One of the questions we asked was: "The Liberal Party's Executive Committee is about to talk to the Ecology Party to find out what common ground exists. Do you think that an electoral pact with the Ecology Party (soon to become the Green Party) is likely in the future? What do you hope would come out of these talks?"

His answer was:

*"I have shared platforms with members of the Ecology Party in the past on particular issues. I don't myself, think that any kind of electoral pact with the Ecology Party makes any sense. They haven't got any effective grassroots organization and they have no track record of success in winning elections or even saving Parliamentary deposits. What we ought to do is persuade member of the Ecology Party that we are a "Green" Party in that we give high priority to environmental issues. This was true of the Nationalist parties in Wales and Scotland. You've got to have a broad platform if you are going to have more than temporary success."* (Steel, 1984)

Within five years in the 1989 European Parliamentary Election, the now Green Party recorded 14.9% of the share of the vote while the new Social and Liberal Democrats recorded only 6.2% of the share. In the 2015 UK General Election, the Scottish National Party captured 56 out of 58 of the seats in Scotland, while being the Minority government in Scotland since 2007.

Considering the discussion before and after the 2017 UK General Election about working with other parties the resolution to the YL Conference from Wandsworth YLs was another indication of where the YLs were politically but also a sign of how much ahead of their time they were. The resolution was titled 'Working with the Greens'. It opened by saying that "most Young Liberals are seriously hassled about the environment." It went on to say:

*"Conference therefore urges all its members:*
1. *To cooperate with the Ecology Party and others in the Green Movement more closely;*
2. *To adopt non-hierarchical, non-aggressive practices in YL branch meetings and structures;*
3. *To support Ecology Party candidates in Local, national and Euro-Elections, where particularly un-green Liberals or Social Democrats are standing;*
4. *To try and hug someone new every day."* (NLYL, 1984)

The 1984 Conference had the slogan *'Sun, Sea, Sand and Muesli'*.

I had spent the year going around branches often on my Honda 250 Super Dream motorbike through rain, sleet or snow to speak or run training days. I continued to publish articles, and support campaigns on acid rain, anti-apartheid, and Northern Ireland.

It was clear the Party increasingly saw me as a throwback to an era they did not want to see again. The Party leadership were busy creating the Alliance between the Liberals and the Social Democratic Party (SDP) – a project that would if it succeeded cement the Alliance in the centre of British politics, not on the left as I and others wanted. It would also fulfil the prophecy that Hain and Hebditch had given in 1978.

As I had mentioned before I had decided to challenge Janice Turner for the Chairship of the National League of Young Liberals (NLYL). Another person who was thinking of challenging Janice Tuner was Mark Jones. He was also on the 1983 YL national executive and he fought a long battle against Janice over an issue which now escapes me. Afterwards he was taken aside by a former Chair of the YLs Alan Sherwell (1979-1980) who spent ages telling Mark that Janice was marvelous and that he shouldn't run against her for Chair – this while her Organizational Vice Chair, Alan Biggar, was telling Mark that he would win because Janice was unpopular. Mark hadn't put himself forward in time to be on the ballot so he turned up at the conference as a write-in candidate. Another of the old guard took Mark into a room to try and pressure him into withdrawing. He said, "You will not win 'cause Janice has postal votes and big boobs," a remark that, had it got out, would not have gone down with the YL Women's Group at all!!

That's not to say that Janice Turner was a bad Chairperson. What she represented was a continuation of the YLs that had been leading the youth wing for a number of years very much focused on international issues surrounding de-colonization. This was an agenda shared by all of us, but it didn't challenge the direction of liberalism or give any coherence to the challenges of the day. Janice had a fondness for dictators such as Moammar Gadhafi of Libya – which some of us were less than happy about. This generation of YLs thirsted to make its contribution to defining Liberalism in the 1980s in a way that the late 1960s and early 1970s YLs had contributed to the creation of community politics and the dual approach to politics.

The 1984 Young Liberal Conference brought out comparisons with the 1971 YL Conference. In 1971 the leader of the Liberal Party was the charismatic centre right Jeremy Thorpe – hardly a radical. He perceived the YLs at the time as a group of socialists who had entered the Party. Others held a similar view while not recognizing that they in fact drew a lot of their inspiration from the great Liberals such as Lloyd George, John Maynard Keynes and William Beveridge who had created the welfare state and the economic stability we had benefitted from after the second would war. The Labour Party of Harold Wilson (a former Young Liberal) had not inspired them, but the Party of Jo Grimond had – or rather, Jo Grimond himself had.

By 1971 Peter Hain and his fellow travelers in the YLs had been all over the news as they campaigned against the Cricket and Rugby tours by the South African teams. The idea that Peter Hain would become Chair of the Young Liberals was not popular within the Liberal Party hierarchy, who tried to stop him from being elected Chair. In 1971, they failed even though a number of secretaries in the House of Commons and Lords had suddenly become Young Liberals, and so, it seems, had some cows in the constituency of Jeremy Thorpe. Peter succeeded in getting elected and helping to identify the Liberal Party for a generation of radicals.

More than a decade later in 1984, the idea that I might be Chair of the Young Liberals was not popular with the Party leadership, either. In a similar move, the Party leadership ensured they added to the postal votes, and it was to be the postal votes that would come to be decisive this time.

Arriving for the hustings and the cheers and loud foot stamping, you would have to think I was going to win by a huge margin. Prior to the Chairpersons hustings there was to be a speech by the President of the Liberal Party, Lord Tordoff, who asked members NOT to vote for me, and said that they should support the incumbent.

His remarks provoked boos from the audience at the audacity that the Party could try and interfere in OUR election. One of our campaign posters were a picture from the Star Wars Movie *Return of the Jedi* with the Ewoks using Felix banners to destroy one of the empire's All Terrain Armored Transports, the four-legged transporter for Janice's imperial forces. The clear message was that we were the good guys against the evil empire.

My speech started with:

*"Today we stand at a cross road for the Young Liberals. The choice is stark, between a centrally run national campaigning group or a locally relevant campaign movement." I ended with a call "Who knows? Five years on we may be moving the Party on once again, from community politics to a new Liberalism for the 1990s. The Party needs new ideas and we can lead the way."* (Dodds, 1984)

It was not to be our night. I lost by 22 votes. I won the conference vote but lost through postal ballots. It was clear to see what had happened because our candidates swept all the other executive committee positions. There were a large number of the postal voters who didn't bother to vote much down the ticket beyond the race for the Chair. They had obviously been given instructions for the Chair, but nothing for the other positions.

*Figure 13: Juliette Tilley*

Janice now had an Executive Committee committed to a vision she didn't agree with, and new members from the *Green Guard* included **Andrew Binns** (now a leadership management consultant), **Mike Hammill** (International Vice Chair), **Juliette Tilley** (now a Professor at a Scottish University), **Felicity Watkin** (now a Doctor), **Stephen Grey** (a war journalist known for exposing the 'ghost planes' which the CIA was using), and **Adrian Sanders** (became a Liberal MP). In light of the election, I had to decide what to do. *Liberator,* the traditional left-wing magazine, continued their attack. Even with me losing the election they recognized the quality of the team I was leading and but couldn't help themselves but to find a derisory way of referring to them as the "beautiful people."

## Young Liberal Ecology Group
Acid Rain would become a key environmental issue for the YLs. There had been some effort through the United Nations Economic Commission for Europe (UNECE) - an interesting body that included all the eastern and western European governments and the USA and Canada. It was through the cold war where transboundary issues were dealt with. They had under the 1979 UNECE Convention on Long Range Transboundary Air pollution sought to promote information exchanges, research and the development of strategies to reduce the emissions of air pollutants.

In 1983 the United Nations Environment Programme (UNEP) estimated a figure of between 80 million and 288 million tonnes of Sulphur oxides were generated per year. Sulphur dioxide emissions result from combustion of fossil fuels due to varying amounts of Sulphur being present in these fuels. Acid deposition was clearly a transboundary problem with about 8% of Sulphur deposition in Germany and Sweden coming from the UK, and in Norway the figures were as high as 12 to 14%. The UK was described by Scandinavian countries as the "dirty man of Europe."

In Canada, over one and half million people had joined the campaign, and in West Germany, coalition partners CDU and FDP, had fallen out over the advisability of building of new coal-fired power stations.

The House of Lords had in the spring of 1984 published their report on the issue calling for the Government to reduce Sulphur Dioxide emissions by 30%. This was followed on the 7th of September by the House of Commons Select Committee on the Environment publishing their report. It calling for a 30% reduction of SO2 emissions on 1980 levels by 1993. The YLs had been supporting Liberal MP David Alton who was a member of the Select Committee with research and input to his speeches.

The report also identified the damage that was being inflicted on historic buildings such as Westminster Abby, York Minster, and Lincoln Cathedral. It said time was running out. The report also recommended that nitrogen oxide from new vehicles should be reduced by 40% by 1987. The response of the Central Electricity Board was to say the report was full of inaccurate facts and it would add 10% to electricity costs.

In 1984 the Liberal Party Assembly in September took up the issue of acid rain. It was one of the big campaigns that the YLs had been leading on, working closely with Friends of the Earth and Greenpeace and other environmental groups. Acid rain was becoming an issue both in countries impacted by it, and in those causing it, like the UK.

The YLs were again shown to have leadership on a key political issue helping to propel it to the front of the political agenda. It would take until September 1986 before the UK government would announce when Prime Minister Margaret Thatcher was visiting Norway that the UK intended to reduce their SO2 emissions but not yet enough to join the 30% club.

Ultimately it would take a Directive from the European Community to really force the UK government to act substantively. In 1988 the Directive required power stations to reduce emissions of Sulphur Dioxide and Nitrogen Oxides. This meant for the UK, reductions of Sulphur Dioxide by 60% by 2003 and Nitrogen Oxides by 30% by 1998 (against 1980 levels).

As I was teaching I was not able to go to Liberal Party Conference as school had started at the beginning of September. My wife Rosie would attend and proposed at the 1984, Liberal

Party Conference a YL amendment to the Third World motion – the amendment calling for the UK to fulfil its commitment to 0.7% GNP for Overseas Development Assistance (ODA) was supported without opposition and the motion was then carried in its entirety.

The YLs also succeeded in having another motion passed condemning laws against secondary picketing. Secondary picketing had arisen where suppliers to a firm that had a dispute with the employer were being picketed as well. We felt that should be allowed and the Conservative government did not. There had been an incident during the 1972 dispute between the miners and the Conservative government named 'the Battle of Saltley Gate which was a fuel storage depot. Few thought the miners would win but the nine days after the depot closed the Conservatives had to introduce a state of emergency and restricted people to a three-day week as there wasn't the fuel to go around. The result was a climb down by the Prime Minister Edward Heath and ultimately in 1974 the defeat of the Conservative government. It also brought to the countries attention an obscure miners leader Arthur Scargill who was predicted by Harpers and Queen based on the victory to "be one Britain's leaders of the future." (Harpers and Queens, 1972) Mrs. Thatcher was the Education and Science Secretary of State during the Heath government (1970-74). She now had a chance for revenge on the unions and the secondary picketing law was just one of those victories.

The September issue of YL News had in it an open letter to all young Liberals from Danny Fingelstein, then the National Chairperson of the Young Social Democrats.

Danny and the YLs had crossed many swords over the previous two years. He opened the letter by saying:

*"Given our different approaches to our political role, it is hardly surprising that the Young Liberals and Young Social Democrats have treated each other with some suspicion since*

*the formation of the YSD 2 years ago." He went on to call for a closer relationship between the parties, but he ended by saying, "Our record thus far has not been good. There is a need for full discussion at all levels of our organization about cooperation, before International Youth Year – an important year for youth politics. This is written in the hope that such a discussion can now begin"*

Figure 14: Rosie Dodds addressing Liberal Party Conference

(Finkelsteim, 1984)

Danny would join the Conservative Party when the Social Democratic Party and Liberals were merged. He became Director of the Social Market Foundation (pro David Owen Foundation) Then went on to be Director of the Conservative Research Department (1995-1997) and in that capacity advised Prime Minister John Major. Between 1997-2001 he was political adviser to the Leader of the Opposition Willian Hague. He began his Times blog in September 2006 and became Baron Finkelstein of Pinner on September 11th, 2013.

## Women

Throughout the 80's one of the strong elements of our new agenda was addressing women's rights. This covered a number of issues from internal representation in the young liberals and the Liberal Party to fighting for gender-related policies and practices in society as a whole. The YLs in the 1980s had a group of very strong advocates who set up a campaign group in the YLs to promote both. I was re-reading the Policy briefing on Women from the 1983 election and it made me laugh. It said:

*"Our Chairperson has been a woman for the past three years and for the past eight months our Vice Chairperson has been a woman."* (NLYL, 1983)

That means a whole lot of different things in 2017 than it did in 1983.

The leaflet had very good policy recommendations on equality, abortion and health care, promoting changes in the education system to equally encourage both sexes, the women's right to choose, more rape crisis centres and more compassionate attitudes from law enforcement and the judiciary toward rape victims. Much of what was proposed by this group became Liberal Party policy and some were enacted at the local level when Liberals were in power such as more rape crisis centres.

## The *Green Guard*

Other than YL News, we didn't have a voice for our ideas so there was a decision to create one that would challenge *Liberator,* the magazine of the traditional left in the Party, which was not sympathetic to our views. Over the summer of 1984 we produced *"New Directions"*, aiming for it to show the political diversity that we had been promoting on the left.

At one point we were hoping for an article from Gerry Adams on community socialism. We did have an interview with Ken Livingstone, Labour leader of the Greater London Council (GLC), as well as articles by Des Wilson on tightening the Green Belt, Mike Harskin on the Ecology Party Conference, Gordon Lishman (one of the old radicals from the Party) on the state of Liberalism, and from one of the radicals who had left the Party

Simon Hebditch, a look at the state of the Liberal Party, Doug Marchant looked back at the Red Guard era, and we had a colorful contribution from the disabled actor Nabil Shaban who was to play the Dr. Who villain Sil titled "New Wave Guerillas." I submitted an article called 'Stop the City'. Young liberals had started to support the Stop the City campaign targeting certain arms traders who were selling arms to repressive regimes. The YLs had been engaged in this campaign over the previous year. The action was to try to block their phones for a day so they could not do any business. A campaign the YLs had been actively supporting.

We also had started to work with Des Wilson in 1983, trying to get him active in the Party again. Des was one of the most successful pressure group politicians, famous for setting up the housing charity Shelter. He had also been running the Campaign to get lead out of petrol. He was also Chair of the Board of Friends of the Earth International. Des was from New Zealand but had fought the 1973 Hove by-election as an anti-establishment Liberal candidate. The Liberals had not contested the seat since 1966 when it had 16 per cent of the vote and with Des this rose to 37 percent, only 10 percent below the Conservative victor. He would in 1984 become President of the Young Liberals and then, in 1986, President of the Liberal Party. Like us, he saw the chance to move the Party to a green-liberal space.

You might wonder why people of a green disposition didn't join the Green Party. In the mid to late 1980s the Liberals and then the Liberal Democrats were the Green Party, in part because of the work of the young liberals and the liberal councillors who were at the forefront of greening local communities. In 1989, Sutton Council had Mike Cooper (YL) on it, Sutton Council became the first local council in the UK to set up a recycling system for fridges to take CFCs out of them and recycle them as the Montreal Protocol on Ozone Depleting Chemicals started to be implemented.

This played into the deepest fears of the Party that there had been an ongoing infiltration of the youth wing by not only socialists but also 1960s hippies and green activists. *Liberator's* review of *New Directions* included passages unprintable even here, and the *Liberator* reviewer even suggested that people should steal my Bob Dylan records. By the way, I still have all my Bob Dylan records. They are safely locked away in a safe deposit box in a bank in xxxxxxxx!! Of course, Dick Flack's one of the leading members of the Students for a Democratic Society said of the Port Huron Statement (on participatory democracy – which Community Politics is based), "To understand the Port Huron Statement you have to understand Bob Dylan."

*New Directions* was the magazine where we chose the name 'The *Green Guard*' because it played to the history of the youth wing and the idea that it was time for a new direction.

Figure 15: Mike Harskin in Asgard

The Red Guard (as I already have mentioned) had done that for the 1960s and early 1970s YLs. It was Mike Harskin who came up with the name.

*"Before the new radicals in the Liberal Party, and more specifically in the Young Liberals, are given a name, we have chosen out own: The Green Guard. The name may hark back to previous eras, but what we suggest, the changes we want to make, and the sort of society we hope to build owe little to the past. We are fighting for the future – an ecological, sustainable and libertarian future. We make no apology for borrowing the YL slogan – fighting for tomorrow – because unlike many present YL preoccupations, our philosophy goes further than day-today political issues. And further than a political view that even amongst YLs is based far too much on Westminster and Whitehall Place."*

The editorial ends with:

*"The Labour Party, indeed Ken Livingstone in this magazine, claims that the Labour Party will be the vehicle to create a Robert Kennedy type coalition. This will never happen. Only a libertarian, Liberal, base for a wider alliance of community and pressure groups, workers, ethnic minorities the disposed and others holds hope for any of these groups. We do not see the Alliance with the SDP as any positive move towards this wider coalition. We call instead for contact and mutual help with a wider range of community groups, ecological and environmentally concerned people and individuals who share our dream."*
(New Directions, 1984)

This was very much the approach taken by U.S. President Obama in his election and re-election in 2008 and 2012.

Perhaps the mistake was not only the above for *Liberator* but the reprinting of the Yippie manifesto (thanks Olly Grender!!) from the late 1960s. This just seemed to confirm to them that these YLs were just a flash back to the 1960s. which called for:
- *The legalization of marihuana and all other psychedelic drugs*
- *The abolition of all laws related to crimes without victims. That is retention only of laws relating to crimes in which there is an unwilling injured Party such as murder, rape and assault.*
- *A prison system based on the concept of rehabilitation rather than punishment*

- *A society which works toward and actively promotes the concept of "full employment". A society in which people are free from the drudgery of work. Adoption of the concept "Let the Machines do it."*
- *The total disarmament of all the people beginning with the police. This includes not only guns, but such brutal devices as tear gas, MACE, electric prods, blackjacks, billy clubs and the like*
- *The abolition of money, the abolition of pay housing, pay media, pay transportation, pay food, pay education, pay clothing, pay media help and pay toilets.*
- *The elimination of pollution from our air and water*
- *Incentives for the decentralization of our crowded cities*
- *Free birth control information…abortion when desired*
- *A restricted educational system which provides the student power to determine their course of study and allows for student participation in overall policy planning*
- *An end to all censorship. We are sick of a society which has no hesitation about showing people committing violence and refuses to show a couple fucking*
- *We believe that people should fuck all the time, anytime, whoever they wish.* (Yippee Manifesto, 1968)

## Asgard: Home of the Young Liberals
I've mentioned Asgard a number of times in this chapter but it I feel needs a little more explanation.

Asgard was where Rosie and I lived in Acton in West London. It was named after the home of the Norse gods – clearly, I was going through a Thor phase in my comic reading at the time.

The story goes that in Norse mythology, there are nine worlds and these are divided into three levels. The first level is Asgard which is home of the Aesir. Other levels include Alfheim the home of the light elves, Jotunheim the home of the giants, Nidavellir home of the dark elves we live in Midgard 'Middle Earth'. Though I am sure to some in the Party we were seen as the dark elves!

The house was one of the early 20th century terrace houses which are very traditional in London. It was a long dark house. As you came in the front you went past the lounge on the left, then the stairs going up to three bedrooms and a bathroom on the right. If you continued down the corridor there was another room on the left which I used as an office. At the end of the corridor was a breakfast room and a large kitchen with a toilet and utility room at the end of the house, then a small garden. In an evening, we would often all congregate in the breakfast room which had a breakfast bar into the kitchen and so Rosie

would potter there and whoever was living in Asgard with us at the time would be in the breakfast room plotting our next adventure.

The house was situated in a quiet neighborhood about ten minutes' walk to Action Town underground and around five minutes from the high street and an old turn-of-the-century swimming pool which still had the individual changing rooms on the side of the swimming pool. One of my favorite reasons for going there was that the roof was a glass roof which made you feel even in England that you were at times swimming in the sun.

The house had actually been damaged by German bombing in the second world war – you could see a little leaning around the roof, but luckily not enough for us to be unable to sell it 15 years later. The house was too big for just the two of us, so at different points different people came to live there. This included in the early years my brother Simon, Rosie's sister Carolina, and a couple of her friends.

It is difficult to pinpoint the time when Asgard became the home of the Young Liberals but it possibly started a couple of months after I had lost the election for Chairperson of the YLs (April 1984). In June 1984, there was a knock at the door, which I opened to find Mike Haskin's mother and Mike himself with boxes of clothes and books. Mike walked past me and into the lounge putting his box down, followed by his mother and both going back to the car for more. This happened many times. On the fourth or fifth time as I was still standing at the door in a dazed manner, his mother asked: "You did know he was moving in?"

Shortly after that, we had Marvel artist John Charles draw and paint on Mike's door a picture of the Marvel character Howard the Duck – which seemed so appropriate to Mike.

For those who don't know the character, shame on you, go and buy the full original series. It comes from the crazy mind of Steve Gerber, one of the all-time great comic writers with a wicked sense of humor. He was also remembered for taking Marvel to court over the ownership of the character he had invented. This was a running issue in the industry which had been highlighted through Joe Shuster who had created Superman with Jerry Siegel. When the first Superman film came out in 1976, he was working as a delivery man. This was embarrassing, and a deal was struck to pay him $20,000 a year for life with medical insurance. Similarly, Steve's career in comics continued after Howard the Duck, but in my opinion, it never reached the heights of those years he did Howard the Duck.

YL Financial Officer Kieran Seale joined us in Asgard in July, 1985, and at different points Olly Grender (now Baroness Grender) and Jane Godden (girlfriend of Mike Cooper, the newsletter editor) also took up residence.

House meetings for Mike were always difficult because they tended to be about something he had done wrong, and the list of his transgressions was quite long. Mike was very creative often producing leaflets or articles or press releases. To do this, you created a master which could then be photocopied or printed. In the 1980s this was generally through using Letraset. For this generation, it must seem strange that you would buy a sheet of letters that came in all sizes. If you rubbed the letter with a pencil on one side, the letter came out on the paper. These were good for headings. You used a typewriter or later a computer to print out the words under the headings. If you wanted artwork then usually this came from a preprinted set that the YLs or the Association of Liberal Councillors (ALC) had produced and you simply cut images out and spray glued the back and then fixed to the master. When producing leaflets or newsletters, Mike was well known for not putting anything under what he was spray gluing so often the floor would be the repository for much of the spray glue. This would become obvious when you walked over it and your feet would stick to the floor. As you could imagine, people were not very happy with this in the house, and this would often be on the agenda for a house meeting.

Because I was a teacher, I was very strict about no drugs in the house. One of those visiting the house often was James, who was going out with Fiona. Both enjoyed "smoking weed," but mostly kept to the rule. One evening we were all in the breakfast room or the kitchen when Olly arrived home drunk and convinced that someone had been following her back from Acton High Street. I wasn't convinced that the person wasn't trying to help her as she was so drunk. Anyway, we called the police and they were very nice. The policeman sat on the sofa and took a statement from Olly – who by this time had sobered up after a number of coffees. As the policeman was getting up from the sofa, I noticed James had left a bag of hash there and the policeman had been sitting on it. Thankfully he didn't see it.

Some of my fondest memories of the YLs were evenings where the house worked together on the next YL project. When we did that, we were productive, cooperative and much of the time feeling we were making our contribution to making not just the Liberal Party greener but perhaps even influencing the national politics agenda. We also had a lot of fun.

## Sutton by-election

I had continued doing a large number of branch visits and training days. To support the training a number of us got together as part of a Young Liberal Collective (*Andy Binns, Fiona Bacon, Louise Harris, Derek Jackson, Carina Trimingham and the two Mikes Cooper and Harskin*). Unlike *New Directions,* this magazine wasn't focused at the political agenda so much as giving YLs material to help them run housing, unemployment and other campaigns in their areas. The magazine was to find fame in a by-election for a council seat in Sutton. Mike Cooper one of the editors of the magazine was standing in the by-election. A *Campaign Briefing* editorial in issue 1 gave a clear idea what this newsletter would attempt, when it said:

*"We aim to increase your activism and work for change…providing practical and relevant ideas, campaigns and resources for your local YL branch to use."* (Campaign Briefing, 1985)

Figure 16: Mike Harskin in his bedroom in Asgard

The first issue of *Campaign Briefing* had a section on direct action and a cartoon of some people digging up cricket pitches, which was a play on the Stop the 1970s Cricket Tour. The conservatives put a leaflet out quoting a saying they regarded as dangerous leftism, which was the idea that Liberals "believe people should take control of their own lives and decisions".

Figure 17: Mike Harskin and Stephen Grey in Asgard

Local papers devoted front pages to this on polling day and the Tories had put out two leaflets in two days highlighting the issue. The Conservative or Tory (as we like to call them) candidate accused Mike of being a supporter of the IRA and member of a militant tendency within the Liberal Party. Their last leaflet said:

*"At best, one can put the Liberal candidate's militant tendencies down to his youth and inexperience,"* (Young Liberal News, 1985)

Clearly the residents of the leafy borough of Carshalton North ward were not worried. Mike romped home with a swing of 13% to the Alliance. His taking the seat also meant the Liberals overtook the Labour Party and became the official opposition.

Mike Cooper (Liberal/SDP Alliance) 1,267
John Stapley (Conservative) 892
Peter Smith (Labour) 412

In celebration, the following song was composed.

**The Orange Banner** (sung to the Red Flag)
Carshalton North - that's part of Sutton -
Decided to elect Ted Dutton
He went about with f.1rn Ghent
When she came buck her arm was bent
Meanwhile a dirty dog, called Stapley,
Went spreading libels all too happily

The orange banner's far too bright
When dirty deeds are done at night

Joan Ghent put out a pure 'In Touch'
Which didn't bend the facts too much
The Tories could not take truth neat
So she gave up her Council seat
And in her place, came 'Honest' John
Whom even liars frown upon

The orange banner's far too-bright
When dirty deeds are done at night

Alliance leader, Graham Tope,
Said we need youth to give us hope
Young Liberals said it would be super
To give a chance to young Mike Cooper
He wields a pretty rotten spade
He wrecked the piton at Adelaide

The orange banner's far too bright
When dirty deeds are done at night

He handed in his nomination
So ended Sutton's recreation
No goalpost stood, no pitch unturned
John Mullin's hockey stick was burned
And Ian Martin favourite horse
Was sold upon the Paris Bourse

The orange banner's far too bright
When dirty deeds are done at night

John Stapley tried to save the world
With law and order flag unfurled
Loudspeakers and a motorcade
And frequent sips of lemonade
But he obtained no satisfaction
From his assaults on Direct Action

The orange banner's far too bright
when dirty deeds are done at night

Carshalton fell to the attraction
Of violence and Direct Action
Both Labour and the Tory voters-
Became a mob of aggro doters
Reclining in the Council _ Rolls          .
Old Tope declared "We vault the polls".

The orange banner's far too bright
When dirty deeds are done at night

Two years later the Conservatives would lose overall control of Sutton Council, and in 1990, the Liberals would take overall control, which they retain to date. Mike would go on to be Leader of the Council.

## Campaign Briefing Retreats

The first retreat one had happened in early 1984 before the YL Conference, but then they were held every 4 months in different parts of the country. They were an opportunity for training for YLs on taking direct action, running campaigns, public speaking, dealing with the media, and related activities.

Mike Harskin developed three popular role-playing games for these retreats. The first was a mock House of Commons where you were given a brief on which Member of Parliament (MP) for which Party you were to represent and what your position on a particular issue was. It was a great chance to help those participating to learn public speaking.

The second of the games taught you how to develop a press release and then put yourself in the position of a news editor to prioritize what stories they would run in a 15-minute news programme. It helped a generation of YLs to learn the media ropes. One only has to look at where some of those participating in the retreats ended up: *Carina Trimingham* (Sky), *Olly Grender* (Director of Communications for Shelter then the Liberal Democrats), *Stephen Gray* (Sunday Times and then Reuters correspondent), *Ed Lucas* (Editor, The Economist) to name a few. I would add myself to that list because I have had to deal with the media when I ran the NGO Stakeholder Forum often. Without Mike Harskin's insights, I doubt I would in later life have been as effective as I became with the media.

Figure 18: Olly Grender and other YLs relaxing in Yorkshire

Figure 19: Melissa Olivek, Edward Lucas and Louise Harris

The third role-playing game was known as the Campaign Game. Here you worked in teams to address a particular issue. For example, one was titled Education for All: Grants not Bombs!! The instructions included the following:

A local Liberal councillor on the town's Education Committee has asked your Union of Liberal Students

Figure 20: A Campaign Briefing weekend

Figure 21: Roy Blockley, Mike Harskin, Louise Harris and Stephen

(ULS) branch for help. He has just found out from the Education Guardian Newspaper that his Council has one of the worst records in the country for making discretionary awards to students. Your ULS branch has voted to campaign with him on this issue. You have one and half hours to do the following.

A.    Decisions

1.    How will you link his Campaign with students at your college?

2.    What actions and events will you organize as part of the campaign?

3.    How will you mobilize students for the Campaign?

4.    How will you use the Campaign to get ULS members more involved in the politics of the town and local Liberal FOCUS campaigning for the Council elections next year?

B.    TASKS

1.    Draft an A5 leaflet explaining the Campaign

2.    Write a Press Release for the local media explaining your support for the Councillor and his Campaign

3.  Write a short article 100-200 words for the student newspaper about the issue

4.  Plan and publicize a meeting at the college

C. OUTSIDE ASSISTANCE

1.  The local Liberal Councillor

2.  Education lecturer at the College who is sympathetic to the Campaign

3.  Teaching union rep at the College

4.  President of the National Union of Students

This approach working in groups would help those attending to think through campaigns and be able to build up a plan.

The Campaign Briefing Weekends were a huge success and a lot of fun held in different halls around the country.

## Political Asylum

The Young Liberal Acid Rain campaign focused hard on trying to get the UK government to accept responsibility for rainfall made acidic by atmospheric pollution that then affected forests and lakes. The main cause of acid rain was the industrial burning of coal and other fossil fuels. Waste gasses from that process contain sulfur and nitrogen oxides, which combine with atmospheric water to form acids. We had had an interesting media activity around the Acid Rain campaign that the YL Ecology Group was focused on. We had decided to ask for political asylum at the Swedish Embassy on the basis of being upset and hassled about what we in the United Kingdom were doing to their forests and lakes with our pollution.

It was a great media idea. I think we were copying some group that had done it in Germany. So, six of us -- Louise Harris, Roy Blockley, Mike Harskin, Stephen Grey (our leading green), Rocky the Raccoon (our mascot) and me -- prepared to ask for political asylum. Mike wrote a press release, and we were hopeful of some press coverage because he had followed up with some calls, and a few journalists had indicated they might come if nothing else was happening in the news.

Off we went to where we thought the Swedish Embassy was – unfortunately we were using a very old telephone directory and had not bothered to call to check. We arrived at a place that now was an engineering firm. A couple of the press had actually gone to the Swedish Embassy, which we did arrive at 40 minutes later to their great amusement. As you can imagine, the story was about us being unable to organize a *"piss up in a brewery"* and said nothing about acid rain. This was not our finest hour.

The Swedish Embassy people were very understanding, and we were given forms to apply for political asylum …needless to say, our spirits were a little low at that point.

# Chapter 4 The Time has Come

*"The work goes on, the cause endures, the hope still lives and the dreams shall never die."*

Edward Kennedy

**Young Liberal Conference Southport (1985)**

Nineteen eighty-four had been a long year, and I had decided that this was going to be my last attempt to become the YL Chairperson. If the election went the wrong way, I would move on to other things. On paper, my opponents looked much harder than they had the previous year. They were Paul Wiggin and Mark Jones, two people I had worked well with and hoped would be part of my team. Both candidates had what seemed to be a good power base, one in South London and the other around Leicester and the Midlands.

**Direct Action Again**
To get to the Southport YL Conference (1985) we organized a mini bus for the London team. It was more of an early Party, because those of us not driving were enjoying ourselves.

For my second speech to become Chairperson of the National League of Young Liberals, I reached back to a famous 1980 Democrat Convention speech of Teddy Kennedy and built around the theme of "the time has come". My speech started:

*"The time has come to meet the serious challenges we face on issues such as housing, education, environment and disarmament. The time has come for the Young Liberals to be a catalyst for addressing these challenges. The time has come for us to create a new direction if we are to become relevant to the youth of today. If we are to prosper we need new leadership."*

The speech then focused on activities for the youth wing returning to the theme at the end with:

*"The time has truly come for a new direction."* (Dodds, 1985)

The previous year I had not enjoyed waiting around for the election results to come in so this time we decided to do some direct action and have some fun. As the votes were being counted, we climbed into the mini bus and a couple of cars and set off for to Windscale Nuclear Power Plant. We had bought a tree and a few shovels to dig with and were planning to plant the tree in defiance of the governments support for nuclear power outside the nuclear power plant. The problem we had is that there was no GPS for ordinary consumers at that time, and so all we had were maps, and where we were going was out in the country. We also had no local people in the vehicles as they were either involved in the count or at the bar.

Have you seen Peter Sellers' first *Pink Panther* film? If not, it's worth viewing as it is a cinematic classic and he was such an amazing actor. The film has a scene at a crossroad where some drunk sits on a bench, and different cars keep passing him, each with a seemingly different animal driving them. As they keep going by and or stopping to talk to each other, the drunk looks at the bottle he is carrying, shakes his head, and puts it in the bin and walks off. I think you get the picture. We weren't that bad, but there was a crossroads where we kept crossing and missing each other until someone decided to stop and wait for the other cars to arrive. Once we were all together, we proceeded to Windscale Nuclear Power Plant to plant our tree.

It was a very dark that night with not much of a moon, though thankfully it was not raining, as we approached the nuclear power plant. I can only imagine what the nuclear police inside were thinking as 30 or more of us decanted and started to dig a hole for the tree. It's difficult to do a Lancaster accent, but the police officer closest to us said, "Hey what do you think you are doing?!". One of us replied: "What does it look like? We are planting a tree!" Someone else yelled out "Down with Nuclear Power!!" or something like that – and others echoed similar comments.

The reality is that we hadn't thought through what we were going to do, or what could happen. The police at nuclear power stations do have guns, unlike those in the street in the UK. Some people forget that it was the left-wing firebrand Tony Benn who had originally armed the nuclear police when he was a Labour Cabinet Minister and was then a keen supporter of nuclear power. A couple of other police behind the wires came to watch us – more amused than worried. Soon we had dug a hole big enough and planted the tree. With a few more anti-nuclear chants our direct action was over and I wasn't too keen to wait to see if they had called the local police – though I did think jail for my first day as the new chair of the youth wing might be news worthy! But I wasn't chair yet.

We jumped back into the cars and mini-bus and were gone and on our way back to the conference to hear the election results. If I remember rightly, all three candidates for chair had participated in the action, so we were in jovial and friendly mood when it came to the election results being read out.

Mike Harskin had been acting as my Campaign Manager and once we knew who else would stand for the position, Mike did a rough calculation on what my chances were. His initial estimate was:
1. Dodds 43%
2. Jones 38%
3. Wiggin 19%

*Figure 22: The author making his speech*

On the eve of the election Mike did another rough estimate. He was aware of who was attending the YL Conference, and added in two write-in candidates. He now estimated I had built a strong lead and he expected the result would be:
1. Dodds 48%
2. Jones 27%
3. Wiggin 18%
4. Senior 4%
5. Smith 3%

In his estimate, I would win on the 4th transfer of votes as Paul Wiggin was eliminated. In Liberal elections, we operate by proportional representation. To win a candidate needs to get over 50% of the vote. If they don't on the 1st preferences the lowest is knocked out and their second preferences are added to the candidates and this happens until the one candidate.

What happened was not one of the scenarios we had thought was possible. I actually won on 1st preferences. I had 54.5% of the vote.
1. Dodds 54.5%
2. Jones 19.6%
3. Wiggin 18.9%
4. Smith 4.9%
5. Senior 2.1%

It couldn't have been clearer that the youth wing was going to take a leap of faith into being even more unpopular with Party leadership. It wasn't only the Party leadership that had a problem but some of the traditional left in the Party who saw the space they had occupied for twenty years being challenged by these greens – and they were also not happy.

The Party snub came early when it was clear that the Party leader David Steel would not meet with me even though I was the new YL chair.

> **1985-86 National League of Young Liberal Executive**
> Hon President: **Dr Hunter S Thompson**
> Chair: **Felix Dodds**
> Political Vice Chair: **Mike Harskin**
> International Vice Chair: **Mike Hamill**

What none of my Liberal friends ever knew is that I had before getting back involved in the YLs actually applied for a job with the Social Democrat Party (SDP) and was interviewed. They in the end decided not to appoint anyone but it could have been that I'd gone SDP, but for the fact that in the summer of 1981 that I received the following:

*Dear Mr Dodds,*

*I am writing to thank you for coming to see me recently regarding the possibility of working for the SDP. In the current circumstances, I do not think there is a post available for you, but there are further jobs coming up in the next few months and you will certainly be borne in mind. At the moment, we are not sure how far our finances will stretch in relation to the number of staff that we would like.*

*Thank you very much for coming to see me.*

*Yours sincerely*
*Alec McGivan*
*National Organizer* (McGivan, 1981)

I wonder what the impact a position with the SDP might have had in my life and for that matter the SDP!!!!

It was a mistake that Steel didn't meet me. Had he done so, he might have had a clearer idea of what we were planning and might have been more effective in stopping us. We intended to move the Party to the green part of the agenda whether he wanted it or not.

After I was elected, *Liberator* decided to interview me – under the title of Dodds 'N' Knockers they started the interview with a quote of mine (that actually had been written by Mike Harskin):

*"Liberalism is a rich cocktail of anarchism, socialism and a strong green strand"* (Liberator, 1985)

My final comment in the interview were:

*"I think there is a major political necessity to point the Party in a green direction and hopefully actually creating local popular fronts that will bring new ideas and people into the Party."* (Liberator, 1985)

Throughout Mike would put out Press Releases that I never saw. I trusted him completely to reflect my views as they also reflected his.

Figure 23: Bill Murray as Dr Hunter

Also elected as part of the *Green Guard* team were people new to the National Executive.

We got off to a strong start establishing or continuing a set of domestic campaign groups on animal rights, disarmament, ecology, education, health, housing, media, women. International groups were on Anti-apartheid, Europe, (east and west), International Development, Latin America, Middle East, Northern Ireland and Tamil Support Group.

## Dr Hunter S Thompson

It is probably not surprising to any political junky reading this book that we were huge fans of Dr Hunter S Thompson. Most of us had read Fear and Loathing on the Campaign Trail. A wonderful book that is perhaps the best example of gonzo journalism to date. Developed by the good Doctor himself it is a style of journalism that is written without claims of objectivity, often including the reporter as part of the story via a first-person narrative. Thompson was the Political Correspondent for Rolling Stone magazine. He made his fame

covering the 1968 and the 1972 US elections for Rolling Stone. One of my favourite quotes of his is:

*"America... just a nation of two hundred million used car salesmen with all the money we need to buy guns and no qualms about killing anybody else in the world who tries to make us uncomfortable."*

Two films would be made about his life – my favourite was Where the Buffalo Roam with Bill Murray playing the good Doctor.

*Figure 24: Young Liberals preparing to board the David Lloyd George*

A later one with John Depp Fear and Loathing in Las Vegas wasn't nearly as good. I mention this because we elected him our honorary President. The media loved it the Party establishment less so. He sent us a big poster of himself playing golf in Aspen with the message on it "From your President with Love and Peace"

The Press Pack for the Dundee Liberal Party conference had Bill Murray playing the good doctor on the front cover.

### Liberal Conference Dundee (September 1985)
The Party Conference happens in mid-September, which is not the best time for a teacher, but Hounslow my Education Authority and my school Harlington agreed to give me the week off so I was going for the first time since 1977. Many of us arrived on Friday the 18th

of September (my birthday) at Kings Cross Station ready to board the about-to-be-renamed "David Lloyd George" train (Lloyd George was the last Liberal Prime Minister).

The long train ride from London to Dundee offered us the opportunity to plan the YL campaigns for the week. Some of the media were traveling up with us, among them my favorite journalist, Vincent Hanna. Like me

Hanna was a Catholic and from Northern Ireland. He had joined the BBC in 1973 and worked his way up to becoming the by-election specialist and *Newsnight* presenter. He would be immortalized in Blackadder the Third where we has reporting on the election of S.Baldrick's victory in the rotten borough of Dunny on-the-Wold.

There was only one voter in the rotten borough and this was the result:
1. S. Baldrik  (Adder Party) **16,472 votes**
2. Pitt the Even Younger (Whig Party) **0 votes**
3. Brigadier General Horace Bolsom (Keep Royalty White, Rat Catching And Safe Sewage Residents' Party) **0 votes**
4. Ivor 'Jest-ye-not-madam' Biggun (Standing at the Back Dressed Stupidly and Looking Stupid Party) **0 votes**

**Majority 16,472 Turnout 1**

On the David Lloyd George, Hanna sought me and Mike out because he had an idea for part of a Newsnight programme on Monday. He pitched the idea that we would retake some island near Dundee that he called "Thatcher Island." I told him that wasn't going to happen, but that we would come up with something he would like.

On the 10th of July, the Greenpeace ship Rainbow Warrior was sunk in a New Zealand harbor by operatives of the French intelligence service (DGSE). Greenpeace had been campaigning against French nuclear testing in the Pacific Ocean. One-person, Fernando Pereira, was killed.

At the time of the Party conference the French had not fully accepted responsibility for the sinking. In fact, the French civil service had produced the "Tricot Report" which initially exonerated the French from any involvement.

There turned out that to be a French consulate in Dundee, so what we planned was a march

on the French consulate to demand the resignation of the French Defence Minister Charles Hernu. We would be led by Young Liberal President Des Wilson, himself a

New Zealander, and the Chief Whip of the Party, David Alton. Around 100 YLs and world media followed our leaders to the consulate, which actually turned out to be a lawyer's office dealing with French affairs above a Tesco supermarket.

*Newsnight* opened with Dundee Town Hall and some sober music and with the Town Hall looking more like a Soviet building. It then cut to the march a BBC film crew had filmed our march to the consulate. To add drama to the event, we had the letter with our resignation demand written in French and Frances Thirlway, a YL from Oxford, read it in French to the French Consulate. Over her reading *Newsnight* lowered her volume, and you can hear Vincent Hanna say:

*"You may not notice the bemused look on the French consulate's face. This is because he doesn't understand French."*

*Figure 25: Des Wilson with Mike Harskin*

The demonstration was covered in the French press, and the French Minister and the head of the French Secret Service resigned the next day (22nd of September). French Prime Minister Laurent Fabius called journalists to his office to read a statement in which he said: "The truth is cruel," and acknowledged there had been a cover-up. He went on to say that "Agents of the French secret service sank this boat. They were acting on orders." (Fabius, 1985)

There was a funny cartoon in the Guardian newspaper or it would have been funny if someone hadn't been killed. It had Inspector Clouseau (Peter Sellers) with a Rainbow Warrior lifesaving buoy around his neck and President Mitterrand's secretary saying

*"Monsieur le Président – Inspector Clouseau to see you".*

### Wapping Dispute (January 1986)
There had already been industrial disputes under the Conservative government. The best known was the miners' strike of 1984-85. The Wapping dispute was perhaps the second best known. One of Mrs. Thatcher's key supporters, Rupert Murdoch, decided to move his papers (The *Times*, The *Sunday Times*, The *Sun* and the *News of the World*) to the London district of Wapping just over the river from Simon Hughes' constituency. Some of Simons constituents were employed by one of the Murdoch papers.

Figure 26: Young Liberal News after our visit

The move had been planned for months and underneath it was the attempt to introduce more modern printing presses and reduce the power of the unions while reducing staff. The National Graphical Association (NGA), the Society of Graphical and Allied Trades (SOGAT 82) and the Amalgamated Union of Engineering Workers (AUEW) announced a strike. Individual members of the National Union of Journalists went to work in Wapping, and those that did were known as "refuseniks".

This all resulted in the sacking of 6,000 employees of the Murdoch papers. Replacements were brought in from the Electrical, Electronic, Telecommunications and Plumbing Union (EETPU). The Labour Party had backed the strike and called for a boycott of the Murdoch papers.

There was an immediate picket on the plant set up and regular mass demonstrations which included violent clashes with the police and many arrests. Simon asked me and Mike Harskin to do a fact-finding mission for him during one of the planned mass demonstrations. I had been on many demonstrations over the years on anti-apartheid, anti-fascism and the campaign for nuclear disarmament (CND) causes, but nothing had prepared me for this.

On one hand, it was like a concert in places where you could buy merchandise from a couple of double decker buses or the many stalls selling t-shirts and other memorabilia – clear evidence of a thriving free market in the East End of London!! On the other hand, it was as if we were in a violent police or military state. The closer you got to the Murdoch papers buildings, the more dangerous it got. I saw police on horses riding into the demonstration and hitting demonstrators with their truncheons. Good thing the British police do not have guns. We reported back to Simon what we saw and he did what he could to counsel his constituents what they should or could do. More than 400 police officers and many members of the public were injured, and more than 1,000 arrests made during the dispute. It is interesting to note that not a single day of production was lost throughout the year of the dispute's duration. The strike eventually collapsed on 5 February 1987.

## Liberal Youth Day (April 1986)

The United Nations had proclaimed 1985 as International Youth Year. That same year, we did the first Liberal Youth Day in Parliament with over a thousand students.

To kick off the year which started in 1985 David Alton Liberal MP introduced a call for a parliamentary bill:

*"That would be given to bring in a Bill to promote opportunities for young people in International Youth Year 1985 by establishing a youth charter giving rights and responsibilities to young people: and for connected purposes."* (Alton, 1985)

In March 1986, due to the hard work of Mike Harskin, we brought another youth day to parliament, again with over 1,000 young people participating. They were there to lobby their MP and also to participate in workshops on the issues of the day but perhaps the best bit was taking many of them to demonstrate and sing songs against apartheid outside the South African Embassy in Trafalgar Square. In 1984 The Special AKA recorded the song which became the anti-apartheid movement's song and slogan – *'Free Nelson Mandela'*.

## South Africa

Young Liberals had been attending the Friday night demonstration outside the South African Embassy since early 1983. It was an example of YL and left groups working together, and relevant because the Labour Party would have nothing to do with it until the police started arresting people. Then Jeremy Corbyn and Stuart Holland turned up as soon as they could get on TV.

*Free Nelson Mandela*
*Free free*
*Free free free Nelson Mandela*

*Free Nelson Mandela*

*21 years in captivity*
*Shoes too small to fit his feet*
*His body abused, but his mind is still free*
*You're so blind that you cannot see*

*Free Nelson Mandela*

Figure 27: Mike Harskin and Vijay

*Visited the causes at the AMC*
*Only one man in a large army*
*You're so blind that you cannot see*
*You're so deaf that you cannot hear him*

*Free Nelson Mandela*

*21 tears in captivity*
*You're so blind that you cannot see*
*You're so deaf that you cannot hear him*
*You're so dumb that you cannot speak*

*Free Nelson Mandela* (Special AKA, 1984)

I would sing the song again on South Africa Day April 27th 2002 at a Party organized by the South African government at the third preparatory committee meeting for the World Summit on Sustainable Development which was to be held in Johannesburg. Still thought by many the best Party ever!!!

Youth Day in Parliament also included free pizzas through Pizza Express owner Peter Boizot, a Liberal. Some of us knew he was also owner of Kettners in Soho, and so we went there for our food. Kettler's was then one of London's oldest restaurants, opened in 1876 by Auguste Kettner, chef to Napoleon III. Its clientele over the years had included Oscar Wilde and Edward VII. When I used to go there, it wasn't unusual to find Paul McCartney and other celebrities eating close by, but sadly Kettler's no longer exists.

By evening we had another surprise for those attending Liberal Youth Day. Peter Stringfellow was a Liberal and self-titled "King of Clubs" who had bought the London Hippodrome and made it a nightclub; in1983 he transformed the place into the "world's greatest discotheque". He had also been one of the first nightclub owners to promote and enable "gay-nights" as they were called then (1985).

For Liberal First Youth Day, Stringfellow gave free admission to anyone over 18. For some of the students from outside London this was a real eye-opener. Few had been to a night club before, and what stories they told their parents. I shudder to think. We were joined by some of the Liberal MPs including, if I remember rightly, David Steel himself.

Not everyone thought that Liberal Youth Days were a success. There had been a less than favorable review after a later Youth Day by the *New Musical Express* (NME) in March

1987. Carina Trimingham who organized that one replied to that review in the next issue of *New Musical Express*. She said:

*"I was amused to read your article about this year's Liberal Youth Day which appeared in last week's issue. I was equally amused when I met your reporter Steven Wells, as he appeared to be a personification of your rag. A rapidly aging, overweight, middle-class skinhead who made rather sad attempts at being 'working class'. For what it's worth I'll put the record straight about Youth Day...."*

This was all that NME published, but then underneath this was the response from the journalist Steven Wells.

*"Oh no you won't you cheeky monkey! If an Anarchist is a liberal with a bomb then a Liberal's got to be a Tory with a credit card account at Chelsea Girl. What? You are wasting your life on probably the most boring political Party in the history of the world toss aside the noxious open-toed sandals and we shall trip naked through the billowing green fields of Marxist Leninism. Cue the old joke about Micky Mouse wearing a David Steel watch."* (New Musical Express, 1987)

Carina was at that time a punk, so perhaps reread the exchange with that in mind Steve all assumed we were good goody middle class.

I would add I had a fonder feeling to Steven's original article *"Lib Sprog Fest"* because it played into the branding I was promoting. The section I liked a lot said:

*"Faced with a choice between Liberal Youth Day and a holiday in Beirut, nine out of ten Prime Ministers took the first plane to Beirut. The Young Liberals are an organization that have wrestled with anti-apartheid, squatting, legalization of cannabis and anarcho-syndicalism but with the big Election looming its brush the loonies under the carpet time, sensible jumper and nice smile time, let's not upset Mr. and Mrs. Reactionary Voter time and its pillow bitingly boring."* (Wells, 1987)

I thought Wells was an articulate and funny left-wing journalist in the mold of a Hunter Thompson.

### Young Liberal Conference Great Malvan (1986)
It had been a very successful year for the YLs (1985-1986) and so I was surprised when someone stood against me for Chairperson at the April YL Conference. The YLs were split between those that liked the green direction and others who saw me as a radical who didn't fit well with the image of the new Alliance. I also still had not made my peace with some

*Figure 28: David Senior and Nigel Ashton*

of the traditional left of the Party. The team and I had had together definitely delivered, but in politics that isn't all that you need. David Senior had a lot of people vote for him because he was popular and liked and not expected to win. Olly Grender had warned me I might lose.

Senior stood on the platform of the Chairperson should not be:
*"a guru bringing pronouncements from on high but as another member, talking to others with whom are held common ideals and aspirations, as well as some differences."* (Senior 1986)

I was reelected by a 10 percent margin (55%-45%), but that was hardly a ringing endorsement of the policies that had been followed. My % of the vote was basically the same as the previous year. It did show that not all YLs wanted a radical direction. This upset me, but it was also an important lesson which I applied in my work with stakeholders and governments at the United Nations that you need to build out to larger constituencies. I think part of the reason I didn't was that this would be my last year in the YLs and so I had a vision of where I wanted the youth wing to go and maybe didn't persuade people that they were being listened to enough. I did make up with *Liberator* in 2013 co-writing an article on 'Liberal Values for a Liberal Minister' with Simon Titley one of my most vocal opponents in those years.

---

**1986-87 National League of Young Liberals Executive**
President: **Simon Hughes MP**
Chair: **Felix Dodds**
Political Vice Chair: **Andrew Reynolds**
International Vice Chair: **Julian Lucioli**
Organizational Vice Chair: **Rachel Pitchford**
Financial Vice Chair: **Kieran Seale**
Publicity Vice Chair: **Mike Cooper**
**National Members**
Roy Blockley
Zoe Bremer
Rory Francis

---

| |
|---|
| Mike Harskin |
| Ben Jenkinson |
| Noel Nowosielski |
| Pete Addison |
| Francis Thirlway |
| Carina Trimingham |

The new greener YLs again reflected in the National Executive with new greens joining *Peter Addison* (who went on to become a director in the Ministry of Health), *Roy Blockley* (a free spirit who died in 2015), *Rory Frances* (who went on to work for Friends of the Earth Wales), *Noel Nowosielski* (who became a poet), *Andy Reynolds* (who lectures on LGBT and elections at the University I am now a senior Fellow at – the University of North Carolina). *Andrew Harrison* left the Executive and went to work for the media this time London Weekend Television (died 2011) whose favorite quote which said a lot about him was "Upstairs for thinking, downstairs for dancing".

### European Youth Forest Action on Acid Rain
One of the actions that the YLs became involved with through the Acid Rain Coalition in the UK was the European Youth Forest Action Bus Tour. Our part of that was taking responsibility for the UK events while they were in London. The Bus Tour was part of an education campaign which was going around Europe to highlight the problems of Acid Rain. The campaign consisted of a bus load of young environmentalists who would arrive in a city where their partner organization would have organized political meetings, educational events or sit ins and demonstrations.

There had been a reshuffle of the Conservative Cabinet and Ministers in May. The new Secretary of State was the right winger Nicholas Ridley, not a friend of the environment. Angela Rumbold had been moved from Parliamentary Private Secretary to the Secretary of State for Transport to become his Minister of State for the Environment.

There was no chance we would get a meeting with Ridley, but we were able to secure a meeting for the leaders of the European Youth Forest Action with Rumbold. Our idea was that while the meeting happened the rest of the bus with the help of the YLs would occupy the Central Electricity Generating Board (CEGB) HQ. The CEGB was in charge of our power stations, and therefore at least indirectly responsible for the production of acid rain.

We had always thought that the phones at the YLs might be bugged by MI5. MI5 is the United Kingdom's domestic counter-intelligence and security agency and is part of its intelligence machinery alongside the Secret Intelligence Service. YLs had been political active in NVDA for decades so it probably wasn't surprising our phones were bugged.

As we were meeting the Minister our colleagues approached CEGB HQ, only to find they were waiting for us. Instead of occupying the HQ our colleagues were invited in for tea and afternoon scones. They were shown a film of how amazing the CEGB was and what it was doing about Acid Rain. What became clear afterwards was that most of the youth on the bus were really just there for fun to travel to different cities in Europe. When they were questioned about the issues, their answers really didn't have any depth. When we got out of the meeting we found instead of an occupied CEGB, a bus full of well-fed youth who were ready to go to the next city and the next meal.

### Liberal Party Conference Eastbourne (1986)

As I have mentioned, the Party leadership had never been happy with my chairpersonship of the youth wing. They saw me as a throwback to 1970 radicalism, and worried what we would do next. To date I and the rest of the YLs had mostly just been irritating, but that was about to change.

In your life, you can look back at events and decide they were important moments. The preparation for the Liberal Party debate on Defence that would be held in September 1986 is one such moment for me, and I am proud of it.

To give a little historical perspective, the Liberal Party had opposed in 1961 the UK doing nuclear tests. At the 1964 Liberal Assembly, it had reaffirmed its belief that the UK should promote disarmament and arms control in relation to nuclear weapons. In 1979, it had opposed the siting of Cruise missiles in the UK. The 1980 Liberal Party Assembly reaffirmed its:

Figure 29: Liberal demonstration outside the Liberal Party Conference

"*total opposition to an independent British strategic nuclear deterrent and the purchase of Trident missiles.*" It also condemned "*successive Labour and Conservative governments for spending vast amounts on the modernization of Polaris [submarine-launched ballistic missiles] without Parliamentary authority.*" (Liberal Party, 1980)

In 1984 the Party had passed another resolution that called for the removal of American Cruise missiles from

Britain. This call was led by Paddy Ashdown, the new MP from Yeovil who had been active outside parliament on these issues. The Party passed the resolution despite the protests of David Steel, the Liberal leader. It was clear that different parts of the Liberal/Social Democratic Party Alliance were in conflict.

In February1986, the Liberal MPs had tabled an amendment to the Defence motion in the House of Commons. The amendment said that the UK should "abandon its policy of attempting to create an independent nuclear deterrent."

The Party had never been an "unilateralist" Party but it had sided with the view that the UK in particular should never have an independent nuclear deterrent. It accepted the US nuclear umbrella. Meanwhile the SDPs and their leader David Owen, were much more hawkish on Defence. Owen seemed to take all Defence policy as a test of virility and in return the Young Liberals called him "Dr Death".

To help bridge the conflicts both inside the two parties and between them and in preparation for the SDP Conference and the Liberal Eastbourne Conference a joint Commission of the two parties on Defence and Disarmament was set up and due to report in June 1986. This would give time for the different political parties to absorb the findings in preparation for their respective conferences.

The Report got solid support from the Liberal Party's establishment even though they were only calling for a "freeze" in Cruise missiles. My response as Chair of and on behalf of the YLs was a full condemnation:

*"We strongly reject the freeze on cruise missiles as outlined in the document. The Liberal Party has consistently opposed the siting and retention of cruise missiles in the country."* (Liberal News, 1986)

The Commission Report had also kicked the issue of the replacement of Polaris [missile systems] out ten years, as they did not view the need to make a decision as an imminent one. It called on the UK to play an active role in working for deep cuts in both the Soviet and US nuclear weapons stockpiling, and opposed support for President Reagan's Strategic Defence Initiative (then commonly referred to in the media as "Star Wars").

In the UK we did not have fixed term parliaments until the legislation in the 2010-2015 put forward by the Conservative-Liberal Democrat Coalition. It was up to the sitting Prime Minister to decide when to hold an election or if parliament passed a resolution of no confidence in the government.

Meanwhile the upcoming election was expected to be in mid-1987. It was squaring up on the issue of Cruise missiles with the Conservatives being for replacement and Labour being against and the Alliance being for deferment. This wasn't good enough for David Owen – he saw it as a fudge. He wanted to take a strong line in favor of replacement and contradicted the views of the Commission and some of his senior colleagues by saying so in public. This caused one of the other Social Democrat Parties founders to write a strong rebut to his leader in the *Times*:

*"When [the] Polaris missile system comes to an end of its life in the late 1990s, should it be replaced? This is not a question of principle and ought not be a test of political virility."* (Rodgers, 1986)

Another member of the original gang of four founders, Shirley Williams also voiced her fury in a radio interview:
*"It does not follow what the Leader said is the same and identical with the policy of the Party."* (Williams, 1986)

In retrospect, if the Liberal Party had gone to the Party conference with the Defence Commission report findings, and Owen hadn't decided to become a war monger, then they might have won the vote. Instead the two David's (Steel and Owen) started touring European capitals touting the idea of a 'Euro Bomb'. That the UK and France would give up their independent nuclear deterrent for a 'Euro Union' bomb.

This therefore offered an opportunity to build a rogue alliance to defeat the ideas and return the Party to Liberal defence policy, but it would need to be very well managed.

The Young Liberals secured through one of the Liberal MPs a room in the House of Commons in what was to be known as the W3 group (after the name of the room we met in). We invited to the meeting key people and organizations who were from the left and centre of the Party, members of the councillors association, the student wing as well as the youth wing, and the Party's think tanks. We also invited key researchers from Liberal MPs offices, including one from the office of the Party's Defence spokesperson and three MPS – Michael Meadowcroft, Simon Hughes and Archie Kirkwood. We did not invite Liberal Campaign for Nuclear Disarmament (CND) as we knew that they would support whatever we agreed but would also if invited make the proposals too far from what we might achieve. In addition, key Lords and the incoming President of the Liberal Party, Des Wilson, were kept informed through minutes and drafts of what would become "Across the Divide: Liberal Values on Defence and Disarmament." The main drafter, if my memory is correct, was Hannon Rose, who was editing a Liberal Left publication called *Radical Quarterly*. From the YL side, Kieran Seale was our main author. The booklet would be called 'Across the Divide: Liberal Values for Defence and Disarmament and would be signed off in the end by and three MPS – Michael Meadowcroft, Simon Hughes and Archie Kirkwood, the Union of Liberal Students, LINK – the Liberal Information Network and the national League of Young Liberals.

The basic argument developed in Across the Divide was that a Party should never stray too far away from its values – if it does, then people no longer support it and they no longer believe it. The pamphlet traced the history of the Liberal Parties opposition to the UK having an independent nuclear deterrent.

The premise running through the document was the defence cannot be considered in isolation, but must be seen in the context of domestic, foreign and economic policies and especially in light of our values.

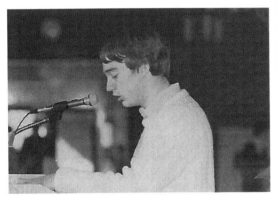

What we assumed was that we had created a process that was very transparent to the Party leadership. We had very good reason to assume this because we had included three MPs and the chief researcher in defence spokesperson's office, and we were copying the incoming President with all drafts. But our assumption turned out not to be completely untrue. No one had told the Party leadership what was going on, as no one supported what the Party leader was doing.

Figure 30: Kieran Seale

The reality sunk in the end of the week before Party conference. Archie Kirkwood, the MP for Roxburgh and Berwickshire a constituency in Scotland next to David Steel's, had to explain that he and two other MPs were rebelling, as was a large section of the Party. I am sure that Steel expressed his feelings strongly, but the dice had now been thrown.

When "Across the Divide" was published that weekend, the Party press office briefed the press to the effect that the "defence rebels were going to be taken on and clobbered."

Des Wilson's excellent book *Battle for Power* tells the story of the 1987 general election. He has an interesting anecdote about how the leadership totally mishandled the defence vote. He said they had agreed on a line for the morning's press conference and that *"overnight David Alton went mad"* (Wilson, 1988). Alton was chief whip, and persuaded

**ACROSS the DIVIDE**
**Liberal Values for Defence & Disarmament**

(1986)

the Party establishment to attack those supporting an amendment based on the "Across the Divide" booklet. Alton was furious because in his mind we hadn't consulted with the Liberal defence spokesman – but we thought we had by having his chief researcher at all the meetings. David Alton puts the blame at David Owen and I think he was right. Owen was getting closer and closer to Thatcher's views and would do so even more when he stayed with the rump of the SDP that didn't merge with the Liberals in 1988.

Across the Divide last paragraph summed up the vision:

*"Our contribution as Liberals to the debate on defence and disarmament, to our Party, to our political Alliance and to the future, it to be united for peace and to be secure in the strength of our case."* (Across the Divide, 1986)

What happened as a result was one of the most impressive political debates of any Party conference of the last 40 years. Not one speaker from either side talked about the upcoming general election; all focused instead on what the Party should stand for.

David Steel had assumed this would be his "militant tendency moment." He assumed it was an assault by the left. But it was a challenge from the centre, and we had kept some of the radical groups out of the tent to place the outcome as close to the centre of the Party as we could.

The previous year, Labour leader Neil Kinnock had taken on the entry into the Labour Party by Militant Tendency. His speech had been one of the best in living memory. He said:

*"I'll tell you what happens with impossible promises. You start with far-fetched resolutions. They are then pickled into a rigid dogma, a code, and you go through the years sticking to that. Out-dated, misplaced, irrelevant to the real needs, and you end in the grotesque chaos of a Labour council (Liverpool) – a Labour council hiring taxis to scuttle around a city handing out redundancy notices to its own workers. I am telling you, no matter how entertaining, how fulfilling to short-term egos – I'm telling you, and you'll listen – you can't play politics with people's jobs and with people's services or their homes. Comrades, the voice of the people – not the people here: the voice of real people with real*

*needs – is louder than all the books than can be assembled (there were boos from some of the audience to what he was saying). Understand that please, comrades. In your socialism, in your commitment to those people, understand it. The people will not, cannot abide posturing. They cannot respect the gesture-generals or the tendency-tacticians."* (Kinnock, 1985)

Kinnock had a big poll bump as he was seen to be dealing with a problem in his Party. Steel thought that by attacking the amendment as "anti-nuclear," it would gain him support across the centre of the Party and, more importantly, with the general public. When the debate started, I was the only supporter of the amendment that was sitting on the stage. I was asked to leave, but I pointed out I could be there as Chair of the Youth Wing. They were not happy, because they wanted a clear visual for the media that the front bench was with the leader.

Paddy Ashdown, who had been the darling of the conference only two years previously on a similar issue - Cruise missiles - tried to find a way to defend the Party leadership, but you could tell he didn't believe it. He said:

*"Let me be blunt, I do not think we can, or frankly that we should, use European cooperation as an instrument to create a generation of European deterrence. I wonder frankly if it can be done at all, let alone done in time to get us off the hook of Polaris."* He finished by saying.

*"Our discussion with the French on current nuclear forces presents this opportunity. It is the job of the Party to open doors. Do not slam them by passing this amendment."* (Ashdown, 1986)

But probably the speech that won the day was given by Simon Hughes, when he said:
*"Where we disagree is in the belief that our contribution - that contribution - should be a nuclear one. Only one of our European partners, France, has nuclear capability. I hope we wouldn't wish to see other countries developing a membership of the nuclear arsenal - a Euro-nuclear bomb mountain, twelve fingers on the button. Fellow Liberals, we could change the direction of British defence and disarmament policy. But we are a Party. Many of us joined this Party because of its aim and its goal: a non-nuclear Europe in a non-nuclear world. We have never voted to replace independent nuclear deterrent. Not only must we not do so now, but our policy must be to do so never - and to replace an independent British nuclear deterrent by a European nuclear deterrent - even if that concept was workable – is not an acceptable alternative.*

*"To work with the French, yes. To replace nuclear weapons in Europe, no. Replacement*

*is not possible for this reason: because the principle is fundamental. Break it once and we've broken it forever. Nobody could ever be certain what would happen after that.*

*"To accept the amendment gives us consistency, credibility and courage. Those opposing have admitted the flaws of their arguments and in their interpretation of the wording. Remember who we represent: Bermondsey, Berwick, Rochdale, Roxburgh. We must be determined that our young people, our children and our grandchildren, have a non-nuclear world to inherit.*

*"We are on the verge of responsibility. There's no more important subject - the battle is not between us, the battle is for our future. I urge you to accept both amendments and the resolution and be proud of all that we stand for."* (Hughes, 1986)

*Figure 31: Andrew Reynolds and Vijay campaigning against nuclear power*

When his speech finished, nearly everyone was on their feet. I was the only one on the stage up and cheering. All the Party leadership looked downhearted.

The final two speeches for the amendment were from Michael Meadowcroft and against Malcom Bruce. Meadowcroft kept to the line that we were choosing a liberal policy, not a Liberal/Social Democratic Party Alliance policy. Malcolm Bruce, for his part, focused his speech on the positions of the other two parties. The speech did not rise to what was needed, as clearly the pro-amendment speakers had won the arguments, and now all we had to wait for was to see if they (we) had won the vote.

When the vote came in, our arguments won the day 652 to 625 votes, a majority of 27. Many of those who voted against us didn't believe in what they were voting for, but were reluctantly supporting the leadership. The vote had taken place at 6pm and so was already in the evening news and there was no chance for a recount as we had to vacate the hall as it was booked for another evening event not associated with the conference.

A line had been drawn in the sand that said politics is about values not winning at any price.

The resulting *Guardian* editorial said:

*"This was a Liberal debate about Liberal policy and speaker after speaker stressed the supremacy of Liberal values over political necessity."* (Guardian, 1986)

After the Conference, the leaders of the two parties got together with the Party Presidents which, for the Liberals, was Des Wilson, and came up with the compromise of a 'freeze' in the deployment of cruise missiles. The wording was very close to what the joint Commission on Defence and Disarmament had suggested. After the agreement, Des Wilson sent me the following letter:

*Dear Felix,*
*You deserved better*
*You've given a fantastic lead in the right direction. Don't lose heart.*
*Keep the faith.*
*Yours ever*
*Des* (Wilson, 1986)

I am sure David Steel was thinking he had been right about trying to stop me becoming chair of the youth wing but the reality is the coalition I helped put together was only possible because of the basic values the Party had and was not prepared to give up. This had been one of my proudest moments working with great colleagues, and it was probably the last great debate of a Party conference as we moved into the 1990s and Party conferences became even more stage-managed. David Steel couldn't stop himself from criticizing those who had votes for the amendment in his leader's speech ridiculing local councils that had declared themselves nuclear free zones. That week the Liberal Kingston Council voted to make the borough a Nuclear-Free Zone. During

Figure 32: Andrew Binns launching the YL Drugs Pack

the conference week local Liberal councillors had driven back from Eastbourne to vote it through and then head back to Eastbourne. The 'Nuclear Free Zone' decision in Kingston was only possible with the votes of 18 Liberals, 4 Labour and paradoxically 4 SDP members which included David Campanale the youngest SDP councillor in the country.

Clearly the two David's were not aligned with their grass roots. Kingston under Liberal leadership through the Leader and Deputy Leader of the Council who were still in their twenties - Chris Nicholson and Steve Harris. also, disinvested Kingston funds from South Africa as a number of progressive local authorities were doing.

## Young Liberal Drugs Pack
One of the *Green Guard*, Andy Binns, had left the YLs. We persuaded him to put on his old YL hat one last time because he had helped develop the YL Drugs Pack which we wanted to launch at the 1986 Party Conference. The Drugs Pack which included dummy local council resolutions, artwork to campaign with, dummy press releases, a list of activities that could be held. The Drugs Pack was covered on the youth BBC newsbeat programme with Andy doing a great job. The approach we took was seeing this as an addiction issue not a criminal issue. The position we were taking included:
- Allowing for the controlled supply of drugs through the National Health Service (NHS)
- Making possession and supply and cultivation of cannabis legal
- Restricting tobacco and alcohol advertising to point of sale
- Obligating products that contained alcohol to carry a health warning. (NLYL, 1986)

Like Northern Ireland, environmental issues, Anti-Apartheid, development issues, peace, LGBT and gender issues the Young Liberals were ahead of their time in advocating policies that are now mainstream.

## David Penhaligon MP
One of the most loved MPs was David Penhaligon. He was one of the architects of the community politics approach, but more than anything else, he was a politician who could connect with everyday people. He had been active in the Young Liberals in the 1960s, leading both Truro and the Cornish Young Liberals from 1966-68.

In 1974, he overturned a 21,000-Conservative majority, creating a 2,561 Liberal one, and joined parliament. His speeches were often humorous and with a strong Cornish accent. He had been the Liberal Party's Environment Spokesperson in the House of Commons. He was always a friend of the YLs and during my time came to the 1986 Young Liberal Conference in Great Malvern as Party President.

David was thought by many people to be the front runner to take over from David Steel if and when Steel stood down. Tragically, he was killed in a car crash on December 22nd 1986 at the age of 42, and the headline "The Voice of Cornwall dies" summed up how many people saw him.

One of my favorite quotes of his – though not one I agreed with - was:

*"To adopt nuclear development would be akin to behaving like a virgin in a brothel."* (Penhaligon, 1984)

I have wondered sometimes what the results of the 1992 general election would have been if he had lived and become Party Leader.

I tend to think that the Conservatives might not have won the majority, and we could have had a Liberal/Labour coalition. I do think that individual people can matter very much.

Figure 33: the author and David Penhaligon

### Eastern Europe
There were many campaigns that the Young Liberals engaged in which I wasn't so involved in myself. One of these was around the encouragement that leading members of the Liberal Party, particularly David Alton, gave to young activists who were making links with the Liberal opposition in the countries of Eastern Europe.

By the end of 1985 as Chief Whip, David Alton had turned the party's operations close to the chamber of the House of Commons into a campaign hub of Liberal activism. The rooms were crammed with desks and chairs and Alton's style of operations was to be in permanently switched-on campaign mode. There was always some extra-parliamentary issue or other being fought and another campaign being planned. Alton gathered the best of the Young Liberals to come and work for the party's MPs. Some of them were even paid. The rest lived on Luncheon Vouchers, cash for rail tickets, the dole and the buzz of being around a lot of like-minded campaigners, having fun throwing various spanners in the parliamentary works.

Unlike some in the party hierarchy, Alton was willing to turn some of the YL goals into action, such as Liberal Youth Day. When he first got elected in the 1979 Edgehill by-election, he was just 27. He was at ease letting his team – who in 1985 were not that many years younger than him – just get on it with what he always did himself, shake things up. Mike Harskin was obviously in his element. He became a key link between the party in the country out doing constituency campaigns – and questions, motions and amendments being laid by MPs – some who even knew about it before these happened. It was a smoothly-run system of getting issues passionate to party members taken-up by the Parliamentary party.

These were also the days of the SDP Liberal Alliance and one of the team David Alton brought into the Whips Office in 1985 – the SDP MPs were based elsewhere – was David Campanale. He also had a part-time role as Assistant General Secretary to the Tawney Society, which had been set up as the SDP's version of the Fabians. But he was best known to Young Liberals from west London, where at 22 he became the youngest councillor in the new Alliance administration in Kingston upon Thames, led by Liberals still in their late twenties. In the Whips Office, Campanale took on the human rights and liberty issues passionate to Alton, but also to a lot of the party's non-conformist and Catholic MPs, like Richard Wainright, Jim Wallace, Alan Beith and David Steel. But it was into Russia and Eastern Europe that Campanale, Alton, backed by Mike, devoted their campaign attention. An underground Russian bass-guitarist and Baptist, Valeri Barinov, was doing time in a Leningrad prison for a subversive Christian rock opera the Soviet authorities didn't like. Accompanying Alton and his constituency election agent Bill Hampson, David Campanale visited the Barinov family in 1986 and carried to them a new Fender bass guitar. The trip also made visits to numerous Jewish refusniks, waiting for their visas to go to Israel.

But later in the summer of 1986, Campanale made the party's first links with Hungarian dissidents when he helped smuggle an illicit photo-copier, unregistered type-writers, food, cash and audio equipment to a Reformed Church pastor who'd lost his licence to preach for offending the Communist authorities. The preacher's son, Zsolt Nemeth, had just finished studying economics at the Budapest Karl Marx University. He began to talk about the student circle that was looking for real political change behind the Iron Curtain and asked David for help to achieve it.

In June 1988, Campanale returned again to Budapest to meet the emergent leadership of the circle, which had attended talks with other oppositionists the year before at a meeting of the Hungarian Democratic Forum. This youth circle now called themselves Fidesz (Fiatal Demokraták Szövetsége) meaning the Alliance of Young Democrats. Some were still students, others had just finished their national service in the army, while others were workers. All had been harassed by the Communist Party and saw themselves as natural young liberals. As so many were lawyers, they took the bold step of registering a new political party. They were the first in the former Soviet bloc to succeed in doing so. They chose to set the membership age limit at 35, until the 1993 Congress, when they realized their growth had taken them further than they had imagined possible.

In 1988, Mike had gone from being a Young Liberal activist into chairing the newly merged youth-wing of the Social and Liberal Democrats. He took up David's idea of bringing Zsolt

Nemeth from Hungary to a fringe meeting of the new merged party's Blackpool Conference. So on September 27th, the YSLD event was called 'Transylania and the Crisis in Central European Nationalism', with Alex Carlile QC MP joining the top table alongside Solidarnosc spokesman in Britain, Marek Garztecki, who spoke on developments in Poland. The event was packed. It raised some donations for the new young liberals and their hopes for genuine elections.

On November 18th 1988, Harksin and Campanale launched a 'UK Friends of Fidesz' to ensure continued liberal support for the party, which was a bogus 'front' to promote connections within liberalism. Just like Mike's and my "British Youth for Hart" which we co-chaired. To remind the reader, Gary Hart was the front runner for the Democratic Party in 1988 until he was found having an extramarital affair with Donna Rice. He had represented Colorado in the United States Senate from 1975 to 1987.

Over the next two days, at the formal invitation of FIDESZ, Mike and David travelled to the 'second round' of the first ever congress of Fidesz that was held at the Jurta Szinhaz in Budapest. At that time in eastern Europe, in their various 'samiszdat revolutions', every meeting seemed to involve signing declarations. Over the next few years, Mike and David rattled off a series of Agreements between the Young Democrats of Hungary and the Young Democrats of England (as they were known, before taking back the name, Liberal). These 'declarations' focused on calling for free and fair elections, environmental concerns, the no-use of Polaris against eastern bloc countries by NATO and helping each other "in the struggles being undertaken by young people".

The first such statement signed in November 1988 in Budapest, gave a good flavour of what emerged in this period, calling for a "Revolution of Ideas led by young people, who we believe have a special responsibility in taking up the challenges of ignorance, poverty and conformity". It also called on Democrats everywhere to back the emerging democratic revolution in East Central Europe. In early 1989, Fidesz leaders came to London and later that year, David returned once again to speak at the Fidesz Second Congress, also giving interviews on Hungarian television and media about links between young democrats in the two countries.

But revolutions have a habit of spreading. In the summer of 1989, Campanale persuaded Alliance councillors in Kingston upon Thames to 'twin' with a Romanian rural village destined to be destroyed by dictator Nicholae Ceausescu's policy of 'systemisation'. ITN

*Figure 34: David Campanale and Mike Harskin*

News asked him to take a film crew around Transylvania and to go to the village. The crew were arrested but David got the story and spoke on ITN about what he'd seen and filmed. So when in December 1989 news emerged of an uprising in Timisoara in Romania against the Communist persecution of a Calvinist priest, Laszlo Tokes, David was again asked to take a camera and film what he could.

So in the early hours of 28th December 1989, a car full of food and medicines set off from Budapest towards a Revolution where the shooting hadn't long finished. Driver Zsolt Nemeth and young doctor Micky Szabo were with David as they went from city to village speaking to rallies of young people and students. At a meeting in Sfintu Gheorge at the trade union hall, the city's 'old guard' was holding onto control of events when the group arrived and took the stage. David's speech – the first by a western elected politician during Romania's Revolution – brought the packed hall rushing forward and the meeting ended in anarchic chaos. Before curfew was imposed, animated exchanges were held over beers and vodka shots on what the young democrats should do next. The next day, the speeches had appeared in revolutionary newspapers being read as people gathered in the main square.

Armed guards were provided in the next town, Tirgu Secuiesc where Zsolt and David spoke to a meeting in the local library. And on New Year's Eve, yet another declaration was made forging promises of support to the emerging youth movements of Transylvania. It's easy to think at this point that young liberals are good at declaring things which amount to hot air and wishful thinking. But Campanale's response to the question of how to sustain the revolution and liberal ideas, continues to bear fruit. He proposed an annual 'political festival' camping week, with music, arts and talks on political and philosophical themes. Nearly 30 years later, the 'Tusvanyos Summer University' in Transylvania attracts 18,000 youth and students annually to a mix of rock and folk music, speaker events, round-table discussions and party-going. It's probably the biggest event of its kind in East Central Europe and a cross between Glastonbury and the Wye Book Festival.

Democracies require elections. Before returning from Romania's Revolution, David talked through with the Fidesz leadership their plans for Hungary's first free elections since the

War. And in early 1990, Mike and David sent over two off-set litho printers into Hungary, which saw the first 'Fidesz Fokusz' leaflets distributed in Budapest, along with dayglow-orange diamond posters.

In 1988 Fidesz was close in political terms to the German Free Democrats when they were a left of centre party, but both moved to the right in the 1990s. Mike and David continued to host liberals from both Fidesz and the Free Democrats in London. Despite joining the Liberal International, Fidesz ended up the European Peoples Party – the Christian Democrats. In the SDL News in 1988, David had written an article casting ahead to the future of central European politics, saying he thought it would be the Christian Democrats inside Fidesz who broke away. It turned out he was only half right – it was the social liberals in the leadership who jumped ship, with some ending up as ministers in the Free Democrat coalition with the Socialists that won the second elections Hungary was to hold that decade.

Why did Hungary and Transylvania become the focus of liberal organization and not neighbouring Soviet bloc countries? The answer is down to the actions of individuals like David – inspired by his Christian faith – and Mike, who was re-discovering his Jewish roots and the people they forged lasting friendships of trust. Then there's the geographical reality of Hungary sharing a border with Austria. When the decision was taken to let refugees leave in 1988, the genie was out of the bottle and the 'Iron Curtain' had been cut down the middle.

In September 1989, David Alton and Bill Hampson heard about a mass demonstration in western Ukraine – then inside 'the Soviet Union of Socialist Republics' and took David with them to film it. The people of Lvov – predominantly Greek Catholic rite – marched to demand the return of their cathedral, which had been taken by Stalin and given to the Russian Orthodox. They were led by Catholics who'd been in the prisons for their faith, who met the British group to discuss their country's political future and issues of liberty. The subsequent film – in a report voiced by David Alton – went on to become the lead story on BBC Newsnight and a global exclusive at a time when very little was coming from inside the Soviet Union by way of film of protests.

"Securing human rights in the new democracies became the next challenge. David and Mike took Lord Alton to Budapest in 1991 and then onto Romania over the New Year. It was partly a hidden pilgrimage to discover more about his own antecedents – and especially the fate of Hungary's Jews. His own family's suffering was not far from the surface but not something to talk about. David Alton organized for them to visit the Dohany Street Great Synagogue (the second biggest Synagogue in the world and one which is family would have known well). After 1939 it was used by the Arrow Cross Nazis and turned into

Figure 35: Mike Harskin and David Alton lading anti-Ceaucescu Greek Catholic dissident, Doina Cornea, Romania

stables by the Germans. But Mike didn't feel able to go and see it – although he knew its story only too well. He didn't go then but he did go back to Hungary by himself a few weeks later and made his own pilgrimage to the Great Synagogue. He had started to be able to lay some ghosts to rest and had reconnected with Judaism.

David Alton often went to Eastern Europe on his human rights investigations – mostly around issues of religious liberty. In a conversation I had with him he thought that Mike would have agreed with Jonathan Sacks' admonition: "Do not ask where was God at Auschwitz, ask where was man". A deeper understanding of his own family's story helped him to ask "where is man" in other forms of oppression and violence directed at the most vulnerable.

Mike knew that the totalitarianism of the Nazis had simply been superseded by the brutality of communism and he wanted to see, first-hand, what this had meant to those who had to live through it. He was particularly interested in the role played by people like Pastor Lazlo Tokes, who was the catalyst for the uprising against Ceausescu and Doina Cornea, the Greek Catholic dissident, who had heroically refused to give in to intimidation and persecution. He met them both during his visit to Hungary and Transylvania.

Although David ended up, like many of those connected to Mike, working in television and leaving Liberal politics, he continues to support generations of new politicians as they train and think in ideas at the Summer University. It was a funny co-incidence that his first TV job was working alongside Andrew Rawnsley and Vincent Hanna on Channel 4's 'Week in Politics'. This was the first British news programme to interview the leadership of Fidesz – Josef Szayer and Viktor Orban, both aged 25. Szayer is now a Vice-President of the European Parliament; Orban a controversial nationalist who keeps winning super-majority elections in today's Hungary.

Over 100 years before Bram Stoker wrote his book Transylvania nearly became the 14th state of the United States. The land that was being considered was made up of modern-day western and southeastern Kentucky and northern Tennessee. Richard Henderson the owner of the Transylvania Company had purchased the land from the Cherokee Indians. He hoped that the British would recognize the land and then allow the allow him to run it as an autonomous territory. It turned out the purchase was illegal under British law so Transylvania didn't become a US State though it is a County in North Carolina. Who knows what inspired Bram Stoker? Or perhaps he was telling the truth about Dracula but it wasn't about Transylvania Romania but Transylvania North Carolina!

### Young Liberal Conference Great Yarmouth (1987)

*Young Liberal News* produced a special Conference issue in 1987, and I contributed an article for that issue called "Liberalism in the 1990s". I said:

*"Prior to Thatcher the political consensus revolved around the argument of state socialism and state capitalism (Social Democracy). Thatcher's philosophy is a brand of liberalism. Her free market ideas have shifted the political consensus. So far, the opposition parties haven't adjusted to this. The opposition to her free market liberalism should be social (Radical) Liberalism. This is something the Labour Party cannot represent."* (Dodds, 1987).

The Conference passed a resolution in line with part of what I was saying. The motion, called Merger, said:

*"This Conference instructs the executive to oppose any merger proposals put forward after the next election and fight for an independent radical Liberal Party and Liberal philosophy."* (NLYL, 1987)

It seemed kind of poetic that the venue for the 1987 conference, which would be my last, should be Great Yarmouth Town Hall, which was also the venue for the first conference I had attended ten years before.

As often is the case in campaigning organizations, after a strong leader, an organization often turns to a person who is more seen as a "safe pair of hands". This was the case with the chairperson of the Young Liberals who followed me, Rachel Pitchford. She had been my Organizational Vice Chair for two years, and I can't remember a political issue she had spoken on. There was no serious attempt by the group that had been the *Green Guard* to stand a candidate though we had a last-minute paper candidate in Louise Harris so there would at least be an election.

Like the *Red Guard* before us, we were bright for a short period and then faded. That's not to say that *Green Guard* members didn't become future chairs of the National League of Young Liberals; both Jane Brophey and Mike Harskin did, but there wasn't much energy around the new Party which would be formed in 1988 when the SDP and Liberals merged, as there had been around the Liberal Party before that. The Green Party was now attracting some of the next generation of young people with the leadership of Jonahton Porritt, Sara Parkin and Paul Ekins.

In preparation for the general election, it was the job of the outgoing Young Liberal Executive to agree about which ten target seats we would focus on, and which individuals we wanted to see in Parliament. You would expect that youth wing of a political Party would only support candidates of their Party. What I always love about the Young Liberals of the 1960s, 70s and 80s was that here was a place for thinking young people on the left in British Politics. At that time, being a member of the YLs didn't mean you were a member of that Party. As Ken Livingstone was reported to say in Robert Carvel's Conference Notebook in the *Evening Standard*:

*"I think there was a whole generation of people lost into the Young Liberals who are basically radical socialists."* (Carvel, 1986)

I think Livingstone was wrong, and that a libertarian-socialist Party which the Liberals could become would have offered a better home for some socialists and, in fact, had been the home for them. The Labour Party wasn't a socialist Party; it was the Party of the trade unions, and it didn't see a great role for the individual.

At that time, the Alliance between the SDP and the Liberal Party had caused problems on a number of issues and a critical example was gay rights. The later years of the 1970s had placed gay rights at the centre of young liberal activism. They had been led by Steve Attack, the YL chair at that time, who had continued the YL tradition of fighting for human rights.

At the Yarmouth Conference, the outgoing YL Executive Committee decided to support nine Liberals and one Labour Candidate, Chris Smith. In the Islington constituency, the SDP had selected George Cunningham, a homophobe. Chris Smith had become the first UK MP to announce that he was gay – other MPs had been "outed" by the media, but in 1984, Smith announced he was gay at a rally against a possible ban on gay employees by the town council in Rugby.

*"Good afternoon, I'm Chris Smith, I'm the Labour MP for Islington South and Finsbury. I'm gay, and so for that matter are about a hundred other members of the House of Commons, but they won't tell you openly."* (Smith, 1984)

Supporting Smith was seen by some in the Party as disloyal, but it had been a unanimous decision of the National Executive, as we informed Smith himself. He was on the progressive left in Labour, more specifically on the Labour Coordinating Committee, which was then the home to former YL President Peter Hain and Greater London Council Chair Ken Livingstone. The YLs found they had much in common with that group on disarmament, Northern Ireland and civil liberties. He would go on in 2005 to also be the first MP to announce he was HIV positive.

In preparing for what would be my final speech at a Young Liberal Conference, I drew from Jesse Jackson who for the 1988 US election had launched his Rainbow Coalition. This was an attempt to rekindle the Bobby Kennedy Coalition of 1968, and an appeal to the vast majority of Americans disenfranchised and alienated from a system that had given them Watergate and Vietnam.

*"The experience of the SDP/Liberal Alliance had been terrible. It had brought into coalition a radical liberal Party with right wing social democrats. It became clear very early some of them did not hold the same views as us on the issues of great importance. Out there are people who agreed with a lot of we stand for they are in the Green Party, the soft left of the Labour Party, and not aligned with any political Party."* (Dodds, 1987)

I took the opportunity to call for our own rainbow coalition:

*"The Liberal Party is in danger of shifting further to the right in British Politics because of our alliance with the SDP, the Alliance is fast becoming the human face of capitalism. The Social Democrats represent the failed social democracy of the past 20 years, and have no real answers for the 1990s and into the next century.*

*"We have many people who agree with us on many key issues such as environmental policy, civil rights, nuclear disarmament. But we are in coalition with the wrong people, the SDP. What we need is a rainbow coalition of liberals everywhere; people like Jonathon Porritt, Ken Livingstone, Chris Smith and Peter Hain. This rainbow coalition shouldn't be about creating a new Party nor joining an already established one, it should be about working together across Party lines on the key issues of day."* (Dodds, 1987)

The speech caused a small storm and was reported by the main newspapers. In fact, Simon Hughes MP was woken up to respond on breakfast TV to my challenge. The *Guardian* ran a cartoon about my speech on their letters page, with a letter under it by Alan Evans the Chair-elect of the Union of Liberal Students, who was less than positive about my speech.

*"Yet again Felix Dodds, Young Liberal chair, has felt it necessary to share with us his intense hatred for anything Social Democrat. I cannot believe however that he reflects the views of youth in general in the modern Liberal movement."* (Guardian, April 18th 1987).

*"The Alliance offers the Liberals s realistic hope of power,"* Evans wrote. *"Therein lies the real fear of Mr Dodds and his small band of supporters. Mr Dodds prefers the world*

*of pressure politics; that is why he chases unattainable "Rainbow Alliances." Mr Dodds claims that Liberalism has no compatibility with Social Democracy, yet seeks to square his ideas with Ken Livingstone's democratic socialism. Livingstone may have many sound opinions but he is certainly not a liberal."*

The Guardian cartoon had two Party officials speaking to each other and one saying:

*"The question is. How do we vote tactically to keep out the Chair of the Young Liberals?"* (Guardian, 1987)

Liberator, the traditional left of centre monthly magazine, couldn't resist a last opportunity to take a swipe at me. Who better to write it than David Senior, who I had beaten for Chair the previous year? The article, titled "Who put the mouth in Yarmouth?" was full of lies (or as we now call it, 'fake news'). Most of the 'fake news' is not even worth mentioning in this book but he did take a swipe at my call for a "Rainbow Alliance" and in keeping with his election address the previous year, said:

*"The outgoing Chairperson (me) instead played his part in the imminent general election campaign, by calling for an end of the Alliance with the SDP, and a new "Rainbow Alliance" with sympathetic members of the Labour Party. Students of byelections will have noticed that such a grouping already exists, and whilst it may not yet have recruited Ken Livingstone or Chris Smith to its ranks., it does have Screaming Lord Sutch."* (Senior, 1987)

For those who don't know, Lord Sutch had founded the Monster Raving Loony Party in 1983 and was well known for standing in by-elections. He had been a less than successful musician perhaps best known for his album "Lord Sutch and Heavy Friends" which was named in a 1998 BBC poll as the worst album of all time.

Much of the fight that the *Green Guard* YLs had in the 1980s with the party was a version of the same fights that the Red Guard had with the party in the late 1960s and early 1970s.

Looking back, I believe I contributed to take a near-moribund youth wing and, with the team of very talented Young Liberals I have mentioned in this chapter, gave it life again.

We gave it a vision, a direction, we created some of the best resources in the political arena in the 1980s> but perhaps most importantly we took up some of the great political issues of the day and won round the Party to them even if it seemed like we were dragging the leadership kicking and screaming as we did it. We played a significant role both inside and outside the Party in the evolving discourse on green issues. Many of those who were part of the core of the "*Green Guard*" who went on to be national or international leaders in their fields. But above all, I think we had fun. We were a group of young people trying to change the world into a better place…I can't think of a better thing to do as a young person.

And then my time in the Young Liberals was over.

# Chapter 5
# Rainbow Alliance

*"It is from the numberless diverse acts of courage and belief that human history is shaped. Each time a person stands up for an ideal or acts to improve the lot of others or strikes out against injustice, he sends forth a tiny ripple of hope, and crossing each other from a million different centres of energy and daring, those ripples build a current that can sweep down the mightiest walls of oppression and resistance."* Bobby Kennedy

# The new left: A Liberal Catalyst

I was in popular demand in the media after my speech calling for a rainbow Alliance. In the runup top the 1987 election the New Statesman asked Danny Finkelstein from the SDP and me to write articles on Realignment. Here is what I wrote.

*"As we approach the general election the mood on the left is one of disarray. The Labour Party is intellectually redundant and seemingly in terminal decline, the Alliance has not fulfilled its early promise of being a vehicle for a realignment of the left. The formation of the Alliance was the first serious challenge to labourism for 50 years. It has opened up the possibility for realignment of the radical left after the next election.*

*Should Thatcher win a third term, the internal recriminations in the Labour Party will be enormous. As the left blames the right for not standing on a truly socialist programme, so the right will blame the left for fighting ona pro-CND, pro-gay, pro-black and pro-feminist platform. It will be open warfare. The Alliance will itself be ina state of flux, as moves by the Liberal leadership for merger will gather pace. But a move to integrate the structure will be at the cost of accepting mediocrity, appeasement and denial of fundamental Liberal rallying points.*

*The Liberal Party must not fall into this trap. What Liberals and other movements of the left need to accept is that only a complete break with capitalism can bring about a participatory, democratic and liberated society. Social democracy is incompatible with these objectives.*

*Liberals do not want social democrats still in the Labour Party like John Smith or John Cunningham, to join what the press have called a 'tri-party alliance' a mark II Wilson party. Britain doesn't need a stronger social democratic party marginalizing the radical left. We must not move towards the dominant European trend of politics, where the centre-right or right-wing governments are regularly elected, Proportional Representation or first-past-the-post making little differences.*

*There is a ready alternative to social democracy: it is now offered by most Liberals, some pressure groups, some in the SDP, the Green movement and some in the Labour Party. At the Young Liberal Conference this Easter I called for a 'Rainbow Alliance' of the left. In reality this is a radical realignment of the left that has been craved for the past 20 years.*

*That sort of grouping could offer an approach based on an enabling philosophy that puts democracy at its centre. It can coalesce around notions of participation, community, human liberation and freedom. A grouping that is not made up of personalities but, like the German Greens, is constructed from the grassroots upwards, encompassing both a parliamentary and an extra parliamentary wing. Thus, it would recognize that most reforms in this country come about from people taking power into their own hands. Groups such as the Diggers, Levelers Chartists and Suffragettes are now mirrored by those in the pressure groups, women's, peace and green movements.*

*There is a new agenda to be written by a radical grouping on the left. The control and ownership of society by the rich must be challenged through the creation of cooperatives, questioning the ownership of land, a social wage and a restructuring and sharing out of work. This agenda is about releasing the talents and power of all individuals for the common good.*

*I believe that the Young Liberals and the Liberal Party can be a catalyst and the focus for a realignment of the radicals on the left. Working to elect Liberal MPs is our priority in the next general election: but a growing number of people in all or none of the political parties the real struggle will begin after polling day. Like the greatest battles in politics, the campaign for a radical realignment of the left is about beliefs first, then power. Because they have neglected the former, Kinnock, Own and Street may be unlikely to obtain the later."* (Dodds, 1987)

## UK General Election (1987)
In the run-up to the June 11<sup>th</sup> 1987 election, it felt strange to no longer to be Chairperson of the youth wing, to no longer being on call night and day and no longer at the centre of many political campaigns and decisions. Many people who have been involved in Party politics or held similar posts talk of depression after they leave office. Well, lucky for me, there wasn't time because within weeks the general election was called, and so I went to work in Bermondsey for Simon Hughes.

The Alliance Manifesto did reflect a number of the key issues that the Young Liberals had been pushing the party on these were:

---

**Northern Ireland:** We intend to secure progress towards a peaceful and secure life for the people of Northern Ireland. That depends on the acceptance of three fundamental principles:
- Rejection of violence;
- Recognition that both Unionist and Nationalist traditions have their legitimate place;
- Rejection of violence;

Recognition that both Unionist and Nationalist traditions have their legitimate place;

---

Acceptance that Northern Ireland should not cease to be a part of the UK unless a majority of the people of Northern Ireland so wish.

The government of Northern Ireland must be based on a partnership between the two traditions. The Alliance welcomes the Anglo-Irish agreement as a genuine attempt to achieve the objectives we set out.

Our commitment to incorporate the European Convention on Human Rights into UK law will strengthen individual rights in Northern Ireland and we would reform the Diplock courts so that three judges preside over non-jury trials; in this and other respects we believe that the passing of identical anti-terrorist measures in Northern Ireland and the Republic can increase the authority those measures carry in a divided community. We also support the establishment of a joint security commission.

We would encourage those who are working for reconciliation in Northern Ireland and who are seeking to eliminate sectarianism and discrimination in religious life, education, housing and politics.

We believe that the membership of the EEC offers not only practical help to Northern Ireland, but also prospects for the long-term development of a confederal relationship between UK and the Republic of Ireland which could offer a solution to a problem which has claimed over 2,500 lives in the last 18 years.

**Shared Earth**

The Alliance shall:
- Increase the share of Britain's GNP which goes in development aid, which has gone down from 0.52% to 0.33% under the Conservatives, so that we reach the UN target of 0.7% by the end of a five-year Parliament;
- Concentrate aid on raising the living standards of the poorest through more rural development, environmentally sustainable resource use, promotion of self-sufficiency, recognition of the role of women, appropriate technology, training and education, making full use of experience and expert voluntary agencies;
- Seek to increase awareness of development issues through more resources being devoted to development education;

- Change the situation in which many poor countries pay more in debt repayments to rich countries than they receive in aid by seeking international agreement on debt rescheduling and cancellation;
- Combine the Aid-Trade Provision and the Overseas Development Administration's "soft-loan" facility with the Overseas Projects division of the Department of Trade and Industry and the Export Credit Guarantee Department into one division of the DTI - help to British industry will no longer be taken from the aid budget.

## Energy and Environment

Alliance energy policy avoids dependence on any single source of supply and is based on:

- More prudent use of our oil and gas resources so that they are not depleted too quickly;
- Continued modernisation and development of the coal industry, including new coal-fired power stations with measures to prevent acid rain and more help to areas affected by pit closures; the power to license coal mines would be transferred from British Coal to the Department of Energy to prevent abuse of monopoly;
- Much more research and development work on renewable energy sources, including wind, solar, wave and geothermal energy; we will vigorously pursue proposals for tidal barrages such as those suggested for the Severn and the Mersey, subject to taking the environmental impact into account;
- Far more effort into energy efficiency and conservation, including higher standards of insulation in homes and encouragement of Combined Heat and Power schemes; nevertheless there will need to be a programme of replacement and decommissioning for power stations which are reaching or have reached the end of their design lives.

## Green Growth

There cannot be a healthy economy without a healthy environment.

We will take proper care of our environment.

Under an Alliance government every aspect of policy would be examined for its effect on our environment, which we hold in trust for future generations.

We will ensure Britain takes the lead in promoting sustainable economic growth and investment in new technologies designed to remove pollution and thereby create new job opportunities.

The Alliance will set up a new Department of Environmental Protection headed by a Cabinet Minister who will be responsible for environmental management, planning, conservation and pollution control, and promoting environmental policies throughout government. Among the priorities of this department will be:

- Powerful disincentives to polluters based on tougher penalties and implementation of a polluter pays" principle for cleaning up the damage backed by support for good practice;
- The safest possible containment and disposal for industrial waste, with recycling wherever feasible;
- Clean Air legislation setting new standards, with tough measures to deal with acid rain and an acceleration of the phasing out of lead in petrol;
- Introducing a statutory duty for both private and public sector companies to publish annual statements on the impact of their activities on the environment and of the measures they have taken to prevent, to reduce and eliminate their impact;
- Protection of the green belt round our cities.

The Alliance is opposed to privatisation of the water authorities, which would hand over vital environmental responsibilities affecting rivers, sewerage, water quality, pollution control and fisheries to private hands. These functions should be restored to democratic control.

## Opportunities for Women
The Alliance is committed to the principle that women should have equal opportunities and in government we will take positive steps to ensure this ideal becomes a reality.:

- We will open up opportunities for women in public life by securing equal representation of women on all appointed bodies within a decade.
- We will strengthen the rights of women at work through equal pay for work of equal value, equal treatment, ensuring that all public authorities and private contractors are equal opportunity employers. We will restore the maternity grant and improve benefits for families.
- We will offer a tax allowance to help with the costs of childcare and remove the tax on the use of workplace nurseries.

> - We will ensure that girls and women have equal opportunities in education and training.
> - We will promote measures that give employees with family responsibilities rights to parental and family leave.
> - The Alliance wants to see more women in Westminster. Changing the electoral system to a form of proportional representation will increase the opportunities for women to be elected to Parliament.
>
> **South Africa**
> Britain should take the lead in seeking international agreement on selective, targeted sanctions, backed by help for the Front-Line States, as a means of increasing the pressure for an end to apartheid in South Africa. (Alliance Manifesto, 1987)

Neil Kinnock had slowly started moving Labour back to the centre and his objective wasn't at first to win the election, but to be ahead of the SDP/Liberal Alliance and therefore present Labour for the 1992 election as the main progressive centre-left alternative to the Conservatives. I shudder to think what would have happened if the Alliance had gone forward with the policy of a Euro Bomb. There was an effective media campaign against Kinnock with Rupert Murdoch's *Sun* running headlines such as "Why I'm Backing Kinnock," by "Stalin."

Defence did play a significant role in the election, together with lower taxes and the economy. The result was a third election victory for Thatcher with Labour picking up 20 seats, the Conservatives losing 20, and the Liberals losing one – Michael Meadowcroft in Leeds West.

There had been some media coverage, particularly in London, about the Young Liberals supporting Chris Smith, who kept the seat he stood for, but only with a majority of 805. I hope that we in some way contributed to helping him retain his seat.

The *Independent* rightly pointed out under an election notebook headline of "Young Liberals in a Labour alliance" that:

*"QUESTION: In which highly marginal constituency are Liberals going to campaign actively against an SDP candidate who expects to win, and for his Labour opponent?*
*ANSWER: in Islington South and Finsbury, where the sitting MP, Chris Smith, faces a knife edge fight against the SDP's George Cunningham. He has received written and oral offers of support from the National League of Young Liberals, who say they have decided to concentrate their scarce resources to help candidates in marginal seats "who we feel are close to our policies and priorities" Mr Smith is one such.*

*"Felix Dodds and Andy Reynolds, national officers of the Young Liberals have visited Mr Smith, the only MP to come out as gay, and pledged their support. They are recommending other young Liberals who do not wish to work in their own constituencies to do likewise.*

*"There has been a history of concern among Liberals in the constituency about homophobic attitudes expressed by some SDP canvassers. As long ago as 1984 the Young Liberals passed a motion putting Mr. Smith on a "white list" and urging Liberals to support him if he was not opposed by a Liberal candidate."* (The Independent, 1987)

This was the last election I took any part in. I didn't know then that my life would change so dramatically in the next year.

After the election, I thought it was about time to join my local Liberal Party in Action and Ealing. Unfortunately, when I did they refused me membership saying that I had supported and campaigned for the Labour MP Chris Smith. I did point out that that had been a unanimous Young Liberal National Executive decision and there was no Liberal candidate in that seat. That didn't seem to persuade them. The *Evening Standard* started sniffing around the issue but fortunately I knew the journalist, **Lesley Yarranton**, because she had dated Mike Harskin off and on, so I was able to persuade her not to report it. Lesley went on to work for Robert Maxwell's The Mirror Group, and had actually been on the yacht the Lady Ghislaine but not that day in November 1991 when Maxwell was mysteriously found dead in the water, seemingly because he had fallen off the boat.

For readers who do not know the story of Robert Maxwell, he was born in Czechoslovakia of Jewish descent and became a media baron as well as a Labour MP. He had escaped Nazi occupation in the Second World War and fought with distinction for the British. Just before his death, he and the *Daily Mirror's* foreign editor, Nicholas Davies, were outed as long-term agents of the Mossad, Israel's counterintelligence service.

Maxwell's death caused instability and banks started calling in loans. Ultimately his media empire disintegrated and filed for bankruptcy protection in 1992.

One of the stories told at the time about his strange management style at the Mirror is the one where an employee was away for the day and came back to find that his floor had been sacked. The legend is that he continued to come to work, drawing pay for another six months before someone worked out what had happened and he was fired.

The Liberal Parliamentary Party and Simon Hughes in particular intervened in the end and told the local Liberal Party to allow me to become a member. They reluctantly agreed.

## Green Party Conference

Prompting the realignment of politics around the 'Rainbow Alliance' saw events at the Liberal and Green Party Conference. I was also invited to address the Green Party Conference plenary at Aston University in September 1987. The idea had caught the media's interest and most of the major serious dailies covered what I was saying on the front page or page 3. The Independent's Environment Correspondent Richard North reported:

*"Felix Dodds former chair of the Young Liberals, calling for closer ties between the two parties.*

*Mr Dodds will call for what he describes as 'a realignment of the left of British politics to include Liberals, the Green movements, parts of the SDP and the non-authoritarian wing of the Labour Party.' He believes this should eventually become a new party, but in the meantime, might lead to co-operation in elections partly to keep the Tories our, and partly to increase greenish representation. Jeremy Seabrook, the writer and Labour Party supported will also be there, with his view that 'green politics is the only force which can bring about the renewal of social hope', though the Greens have less hopes of wooing socialists."* (North, 1987)

## Should Simon Hughes MP be the leader of the merged SDP and Liberals?

In August 1987 at Asgard we convened a dinner for Simon Hughes to investigate if he should throw his hat into the leadership race for the head of the new merged Party. On one side were Simon's staff, and on the other were some of the *Green Guard*: Mike Harskin, Mike Cooper, Olly Grender, Kirren Seale, Rosie Dodds, and Stephen Grey. Mike Harskin, as he so brilliantly did on many occasions, had provided us with a nice paper to kick the discussion off. It was headed PERSONAL AND CONSTITUENCY INTEREST ARGUMENTS

On the 'ADVANTAGES' Side
1. SH could be leader
2. SH marker for future (next) leadership election
3. Natural progress in promoting SH personal and political priorities
4. SH higher profile win or loss
5. SH as leader much more secure in Southwark and Bermondsey (more secure even if not elected leader – due to higher profile)

6. More resources as leader for SH and for S&B
7. Higher profile for S&B and its problems
8. More clout in getting S&B problems solver (advantage if Privy Councillor rights in Hoc)
9. More help at elections. More incentive to move to S&B more donations

On the 'DISADVANTAGES' Side:
1. SH could lose. Depressing?
2. Poor performance could damage future chances
3. Unnecessary burden and distraction from addressing political priorities
4. More intrusion into time and private life etc
5. Possibility of inducing even bigger effort to dislodge SH (as leader) if S&B seen a possible gain for Labour (very unlikely to unseat leader)
6. More tasks and duties may overwhelm even a larger staff base
7. Possible imagine problem of leader's seat with so many problems
8. Less time for casework and less time for individual cases. Leader cannot appear parochial all the time
9. Less time in constituency at elections. More speaking engagements, tours elsewhere
10. Jobs for the boys (Felix, Mike, Carina etc) (Dodds, 1987)

After a robust discussion, Simon decided not to put his hat in the ring for the 1988 leadership election. In the end, it became a contest between Paddy Ashdown and Alan Beith, which Ashdown won overwhelmingly (72-28 percent). I think Simon was wrong not to stand, as it would have created a great debate around green issues. It would be nearly 20 years before he did stand for leader in 2006 and his campaign and the election were dogged with sex scandals. The final result then was Campbell 44.7 percent, Chris Hulne 32.7 percent, and Hughes 23.2 percent.

In an interesting footnote to David Steel not standing for leader of the new Party, Andrew Rawnsley, former sidekick to Vincent Hanna on TV and now a well-established political analyst is his own right, commented drily:

*"They toasted him, stood and applauded. He sat with his head dipped, his eyes slightly wet. It deserved a song. And now the end was near, he faced the final ovation. Policies, he'd had a few, but then again too few to mention. But more, much more than this, he did it the middle way."* (Rawnsley, 1988)

Years of fighting David Steel and his leadership from the Young Liberals and in particular within the YLs the *Green Guard* now there was a chance for a leader who would be more inclined to our policy suggestions. Paddy – the new leader of the Party was kind enough in 1992 to write a reference for me as Party Leader – something David Steel would never have done:

*"Felix Dodds has previously been National Chair of the Young Liberals and a long-term member of the Liberal and Liberal Democrat Party.*

*"He has been an advisor to me on environmental issues and I have valued his assistance, knowledge and campaigning skills. He has also been at the head of the campaigns in Britain and the Earth Summit.*

*"I would not hesitate to recommend Felix as a campaign worker. He will be a valuable and astute member of anyone's campaign team."* (Ashdown, 1992)

### Green Voice 1987-1988
The speech I ended my Young Liberal chairpersonship with did win some positive response from greens and socialists as well as many within the soon-to-be-merged Social and Liberal Democrat Parties. I and some of the *Green Guard* started to meet with Green Party leaders Jean Lambert, Tim Cooper, and Liz Crosbie to discuss how to take forward several ideas on a common progarmme of green issues.

We decided what was needed was a number of very focused things:

1. Articles in left leaning newspapers and magazines
2. A set of conferences where greens and liberals could meet and discuss common agenda items.
3. A book

Articles were written and published in *The Guardian*, the *New Statesman* and green publications.

The first Green Voice Conference was held in London on 16th of January 1988 at the London School of Economics. The Conference was held before the new merged Social and Liberal Democrats had been agreed – which would be on 3 March.

Its main plenary speaker would be Simon Hughes MP he said;

*"For me the new Party is only an acceptable Party it is truly environmentalist and internationalist; truly devolutionary and communitarian; truly redistributive of our unjustly shared resources; mutually respectful and determined to achieve justice. For me*

*Figure 36: Michael Meadowcroft*

*pacifists and unilateralists; those who believe in a sustainable economy and no growth; those who believe in the abolition of national boundaries and national armies; those who believe in the fundamentally shared possession that is land and the wrongness of private land ownership; those who opposed to inherited wealth and to consumer dominated demand led economics; all must be embraced and welcomed." He then went further and said "Unless these ideals of peace, internationalism and justice are incorporated unto and welcome in the new Party, then many liberals, I guess, will not be able to join."* (Hughes, 1988)

He then went on to repeat this at the press conference, that he would not join the new Social and Liberal Democrats Party unless it was to accept a strong green agenda. Such an announcement with a few weeks of the Party conference and during the negotiations for a new Party ensured media coverage and the BBC had it as its number two item on its evening news.

The second conference would be in Leeds 26-27th of March to ensure that the discussion and debate would not be London centric. Leading that from the YL side for this event were *Jane Brophy* and *Eduardo Gonçalves*. My book on the realignment of British politics around a green agenda would be out for the Conference.

Speakers included Simon Hughes MP, Michael Meadowcroft MP who was not to join the new Social and Liberal Democrat Party, Freda Meisseur-Blau an Austrian Green MP, Sara Parkin joint Secretary of the European Greens, and Jean Lambert. The conference slogan was "Where the People Lead – The Leaders Will Follow".

I remember sitting next to Michael Meadowcroft who had been the Leeds West MP as he was preparing to speak. He got out a box of cards. Each card had a number and a theme, and he went through the cards while the audience was getting seated, picking 5 or 6 out, and there was his speech. It was amazing way of doing it – or so I thought at the time and have used myself many times since. If you have your key points on all the different subjects you might speak on then you can create a speech very easily. The second conference was also a great event, not so much covered by the national press this time. Leeds is a little far for them to go.

In my speech, I said:

*"Greens, Liberals and socialists can work together more openly on the most urgent problems facing their communities. The future is in our hands rather than those of the Party leaders and the crisis of peace versus war, development versus despair, and sustainability versus annihilation are ours to solve. It is increasingly clear that the established parties are unable to meet these challenges and a realignment of the kind we argue for cannot be postponed."* (Dodds, 1988)

Peter Hain, former Chair of National League of Young Liberals and now a member of the Labour Party who would hold many posts, including Secretary of State for Wales under the Tony Blair government had similar ideas. In a March 1988 article in *The Guardian*, he said:

*"Out of the merger (SDP and Liberals) fiasco there could be a real opening for a new realignment of the left involving radical Liberals, the Greens, independents from single issue groups and Labour's libertarian socialists."* (Hain, 1988)

Sound familiar?

There is no question in my mind that foundations were laid in those years for much more collaboration and cooperation between the parties and their members around issues such as nuclear power, acid rain, development aid, local sustainability, CFCs and some economic policies. Some cooperation happened, but the hopes of the Green Voice conference were never realized and could, I believe, have provided a different approach to politics.

I left teaching after seven wonderful years in August to take up a position as the Regional Officer for London for the United Nations Association of the UK. One of the requirements of the position was that you were "nonpartisan," so the Green Voice Conference would turn out to be my final one as an organizer.

### Robin Dodds

One of the two most important dates in my life was when my son Robin was born (the other was when my daughter Merri was born). Rosie and I decided he would be called Robert (after Robert Kennedy), Elliott (after the Liberal philosopher Elliott Dodds) and

Merlin (because he was magic). He was born on the 6<sup>th</sup> of February 1988, and after all those names we found ourselves calling with Robin (after Batman and Robin). I was amazed when he told me he got through nearly the whole of secondary school without anyone finding out one of his names was Merlin. Rosie which I perhaps should mention was a liberal Protestant and I a not practicing Catholic. So it seemed only appropriate that we had a special welcoming of him to this world at the Essex Unitarian Church in Kensington with friends and family in attendance. The Reverend Francis Simons was our guy for the event. We started with candle lighting and then Rosie and I spoke the lines of the poet Siegfried Sassoon:

Your little flame of life we guard
For the long night that must be hard:
Your eyes we teach to know the day
That shall make wonderful your way.

Bright be your flame, my little one,
Whose pilgrimage we see begun:
And when these guiding hands are gone,
In love of all things good go on.

The affirmation was speaking the UN's Rights of Children and after each right read out by the Minister, those attending would say "This we believe and affirm."

The right to affection, love and understanding.
The right to free education
The right to adequate nutrition and medical care
The right to full opportunity for play and recreation
The right to a name and nationality
The right to special care, if handicapped
The right to be among the first to receive relief in times of disaster
The right to be useful member of society and to develop individual abilities
The right to be brought up in a spirit of peace and universal kinship
The right to enjoy these rights regardless of race, colour, sex, religion or social origin.
We also enjoyed some great music with the help of Simon Hughes the Liberal MP on guitar. Now it would be a time of dinosaurs and trains.

## Into the twenty-first century (1988)
One of my last real outings into UK politics was my first book. *'Into the 21<sup>st</sup> Century: An Agenda for Political Realignment'*. Jon Carpenter, who had been asked by Marshall Pickering Publishing Company to create a green imprint did so with Green Print. Jon who

I had met at a number of events such as Green Party and Green Voice Conferences asked if I wanted to develop my theme of cross-Party collaboration into a book.

The idea excited me on a number of levels. First, I had also always wanted to write a book on the themes I had been articulating as Chairperson of the YLs. These themes included, Liberal and Green values; the environmental crisis, the need for a new green economy, and a strategy for working together on the left in British politics. Second, it allowed me to develop my ideas with others in a more coherent way. Finally, it allowed me to challenge dyslexia.

So, what would my Rainbow Alliance book look like? From the Labour Party, I secured Peter Hain (MP), Simon Hebditch and Peter Tatchell. From the Green Party, I recruited Liz Crosbie, Tim Cooper, Jonathon Porritt, Sara Parkin, Jean Lambert (MEP) and Petra Kelly (German Green Leader and MP). From the Liberal Party, I secured Simon Hughes (MP), Michael Meadowcroft (MP) and Mike Harskin. I rounded out the roster of contributors with three independent thinkers on the left: Meg Beresford, Jeremy Seabrook and Hilary Wainwright.

In the review in Liberal News it was one of the first books that started to recognize that there was a:

*"growing healthy disrespect towards the old power structures. People are less likely to trust the media for a completely honest and even-handed view of events. They are less likely to put total faith in every policing or judicial policy. They are more cynical towards the 'we know best' merchants in the medical and legal professions or the we know everything scientists and technocrats who ran riot through the 1960s and 1970s. Most of all, more people are ready to fight back and challenge what they feel to be wrong."* (Liberal News, 1988)

The book would cause a small media storm because Simon Hughes MP and Peter Tatchell had both contributed chapters to it.

Peter Tatchell would eventually leave the Labour Party and join the Greens. When asked during the Liberal Democratic leadership election in 2006 if he had forgiven Hughes, he said:

*"Simon benefited from these dirty tricks, but that was 23 years ago—I don't hold a grudge. It's time to forgive and move on. Simon Hughes should be judged on his 23-year record as an MP and that "if I were a Lib Dem member, I would vote for Simon Hughes as Party leader."* (Tatchell, 2006)

In the 2010 General Election campaign, Tatchell encouraged tactical voting for the Liberal Democrats.

I and other people associated with the book and the Green Voice Conferences wrote a lot in that time period between 1987 and the end of 1988. For the Green Line magazine Tim Cooper of the Green Party and I both wrote complementary articles on the issues where we felt there was possibility of collaboration. I said:

*"This group should have a parliamentary and an extra-parliamentary wing encompassing the Liberal Strategy of the dual approach to politics. It would recognize that over the last eight years the most effective opposition to the Tory government has come from pressure groups, not political parties. It would recognize the significant contribution Non-Violent Direct Action has made in this country; when people are prepared to take power into their hands, then change is possible. One has only to remember the suffragettes, [as well as] the civil rights, peace, and environmental movements to see that."*

Figure 37: The author waiting for his next challenge

*"This grouping should offer an approach based on an enabling philosophy that puts democracy at its centre, as Anthony Barnett argued in The Guardian, that can coalesce around notions of participation, community, human liberation, and freedom. Our ideal would be similar to that of [19th-century Russian anarchist Mikhail] Bakunin, who said: "We want to reconstruct society not from the above down, with the help of some kind of authority and of socialist engineers and other scholars, but from below up."*

*"There is a new political agenda to be written by a radical grouping on the left in opposition to Thatcherism: one that will bring into question our whole lifestyle and our relationship with the planet we live on. It should question the ownership and control of our society by the rich and privileged, be prepared to introduce social income, and to restructure and share out work. Such an agenda is about releasing the talents and powers of all the people for the common good."* (Dodds, 1988)

The book received good reviews on the left, but it was time for me to move on from Party politics. I had been involved for 14 years and had no interest in being an MP, Councillor or Party official. I would write occasionally for Liberal magazines and newspapers, this included a new one set up by my friend David Boyle called New Democrat International (NDI). In its November/December 1990 issue I teamed up with Lesley Yarranton former Daily Mirror journalist and now a Deputy Editor of NDI on an article Towards a post-industrial politics.

## Towards a post-industrial politics

As the 1990s start, growing numbers of people are realising that politics is going through a sea change. There is a new agenda evolving which appears to be based on democracy, the environment and personal not material development.

A transformation into a post-industrial age has been talked about for the past 20 years, ever since the Club of Rome first set the agenda for a new ecological awareness with its Blueprint for Survival report in 1970. It is only now beginning to be taken seriously by those in power.

As we approach the new millennium we are beginning to see a significant move, a so-called paradigm shift, from the old economic battleground of socialism vs. capitalism that has spanned the 20th century and has caused so many of the problems that we now face.

The new politics that are evolving require an awareness of the world as 'global village': idealism has re-entered the debate in international forums like the United Nations.

It was in a United Nations Development Programme report this year that the concept of measuring a country's strength by the standard of health and education enjoyed by its people - known as a country's 'human development index' - rather than in economic terms as Gross National Product, was put forward.

In scientific terms, the old Newtonian dominance is falling away to a new 'chaos' theory, as we realise that we can no longer predict future events absolutely.

As author Stephen Hawking conjectured, the movement of a butterfly's wings in China can affect weather patterns in the UK: we are all interconnected. This unpredictability has required scientists to go back to basics and re-evaluate their findings and methods of deduction.

The answers offer a new perspective on the whole UK political spectrum.

In terms of this new agenda the present Conservative government is a dinosaur - a relic of the old politics that it has promoted so successfully for 11 years. It is committed to an unsustainable form of growth and has little real interest in democracy, having cut away power from local authorities, trade unions and ordinary people.

But the next few years could see a dramatic change in the party. Having promoted the uninhibited growth of the free market, there is now clearly a need, as stated by environment minister Chris Patten, to do what the Conservatives vowed never to do - intervene in the market place.

This makes Chris Patten the hope for the Conservation Party. He clearly understands the major environmental problems facing us - global warming, ozone depletion, resource scarcity and population growth.

Almost a year has passed since the Department of the Environment crossed a new threshold in environmental awareness with publication of the Pearce Report, named after its author Professor David Pearce and officially known as Blueprint for a Green Economy.

The Pearce report was a first step towards basing the structure and planning for our national economy on environmental considerations.

It states: 'The economic principles underlying the "proper" pricing of goods and services and of natural resources are the same. Prices should reflect the true social costs of production and use.

Essentially this means getting the true value of environmental services reflected in prices rather than having them treated as free goods'.

Patten has long been on the 'wet' side of the party with his credentials. Should he inherit the leadership of the Conservative Party from Mrs. Thatcher the party may make a major shift towards the 'new politics' required to be a major player in the 21st Century.

The Labour Party has a major problem with the unfolding agenda of the 1990s.

It has already rediscovered 'Butskellism', and is some way from understanding that the politics of growth and industrialism are on the wane. It is difficult for the party of the trade unions and of manufacturing industry.

After 11 years of Thatcher government, it has committed itself to a market economy, thrown out its policy on Unilateral nuclear disarmament and is now not prepared to say anything that could damage its electability.

The Labour Party conference this year passed a motion to set up a working party to look into electoral reform for the House of Commons: it is continuing to move towards a more democratic position.

The politics of the 1990s challenges the roots of both the Labour and policies.

In many ways, Roy Hattersley shares the same position as Chris Patten. The difference is that Chris Patten is moving towards the new politics enthusiastically while Hattersley seems to be dragged, kicking and screaming.

At the Labour conference this year he continued to show his distaste for more exacting forms of democracy: 'The Labour party is never going to accept PR... I am passionately and intellectually opposed to PR'.

But the pro-growth 'social democrats are not the only intellectual strands in the Labour Party. Ken Livingstone has been instrumental in putting forward a strong democratic socialist tradition, but also an argument that the Labour Party's economic base is not just wrong but unsustainable.

As Livingstone said: 'Labour has it is so old fashioned: even though Kinnock was young and used to a lot of modern techniques, the message was stunningly 1950s. And there is no 1980s
or 1990s message that is not green ... the impact of feminism and environmentalism on my politics and my lifestyle is overwhelmingly more important than anything that happens in the Labour Party and has been for the last 15 or 20 years.'

The Liberal Democrats have inherited the old Liberal Party commitment to democracy but have not yet seriously questioned the principle of putting freedom first, which old Liberals hold dear.

They are also committed to the notion of free trade, though free trade has never existed other than as an ideal. There is some new thinking of replacing it with 'fair trade'.

Former Liberal leader David Steel has often been accused of representing the old social democratic tradition, which others feel have slowed down the growth of new politics in the party.

Despite this, two years into Steel's leadership, grass roots members at the party's annual conference managed to push through a policy committing the party to a non-growth economic policy.

The Liberals were a good 11 years ahead of their time. Bermondsey MP Simon Hughes has been the leading parliamentary voice in setting out a new agenda.

'The political battles for the future will be, on the one side the politics of liberty, community and sustainability and, on the other side, the politics of inequality and arbitrary self-interest,' he wrote in a 1988 issue of the Young Liberal magazine Campaign Briefing.

He has maintained this position since and this year, as the party's environment spokesman, put forward a radical plan to re-structure the party's policy-making decisions around an environmental perspective.

The details were set out in a document entitled What Price our Planet? describing ways in which all levels of society could interact with each other in an environmentally responsible way.

Today the Liberal Democrat constitution recognises that environmental awareness should make up an integral part of all areas of policy.

That message is contained in the preamble to the constitution:

'We believe that each generation is responsible for the fate of the planet by safeguarding the balance of nature and the environment for the long-term continuity of life in all its forms.'

This fundamental awareness of the need for an ecological perspective puts the Liberal Democrats in a position to emerge as a major political force in the 1990s.

Until now, members of the Green Party have led the philosophical debate. Jonathon Porritt, more than anyone else, has set the agenda by which other parties and the lifestyles of ordinary people will be judged.

In his book Seeing Green he outlined the minimum criteria for being 'green'. This included:
- A rejection of materialism and the destructive values of industrialism;
- Protection of the environment as a precondition of a healthy society;

- An emphasis on socially-useful, personally rewarding work enhanced by human-scale technology and open participatory democracy at every level of society;
- An emphasis on self-reliance and decentralised communities;
- A recognition of future generation' rights in use of all resources.

After the Conservatives' fourth election victory, the Labour Party's fourth crushing defeat - assuming that is what happens - there will be opportunities for a serious realignment around the politics of the new age.

There exists a clear set of directions held by members of the Labour, Liberal Democrat and Green parties and by many people who feel that the present political groupings do not represent their ideals.

These include Ken Livingstone, Chris Smith; Paddy Ashdown, Simon Hughes, Sara Parkin and Jonathon Porritt, who together could form the nucleus of the new political movement needed to take us into the 21st century.

### Loss of a dear friend and Liberal rebel - Death of Mike Harskin

I had seen Mike just after coming back from the 1992 UN Earth Summit held in Rio in late June and we had talked about perhaps working together on another book. I was no longer a member of the Liberal Party, and so our paths didn't cross much. He was now editor of *Liberal News* and enjoying it. He was also councillor in Brent and Prospective Parliamentary Candidate (PPC) for the Brent constituency. It would become a seat the Liberals would win in 2003 with Sarah Teather taking it from Labour. Mike's office was like his bedroom when he had been living with Rosie and me, meaning it had papers everywhere and spray glue on the floor.

Stephan Grey was living with Mike in Brent and we got a call from him to say he had just come home and found Mike dead. Mike was only 28. Kieran and I rushed over and arrived before the ambulance. For me it was the first dead body I had seen, and it was clear Mike was no longer there.

Death is never easy. When Mike died, I hadn't been around many people close to me who had died. Until then, my grandparents were the closest people to me who had died.

The police and ambulance arrived shortly afterwards. There was a strange moment when the police saw one of the framed pictures on Mike's wall was of the police dragging him out of the Brent Council Chamber. He had tried to speak on an issue that had been already voted on, and the Conservatives called the police when Mike complained. Mike's response was:

*"If this happens if a councillor wants to ask a question God help anyone who tried to make a speech."*

Loss affects all people differently. Mike was a very important person in my life, a close friend who had helped shape my political thinking and who was fun to work with. I have found that I think of him often when I am working. I had so many memories of working with Mike that even now there will be a moment I will do something and it will remind me of him. He always had this knack when giving a speech and being able to rein it back in after it had spiraled off in an unpredicted and not planned way. He could restore focus to the speech while making what he had said before relevant. I have found myself in similar places and smiling as I remember Mike getting himself out of them. I still have on my bookcase the photo of us in the National Liberal Club when we were young and about to take on the world and make it a better place.

Kieran and Stephen working with Rachel and Lesley took charge of organizing the celebration of Mike's life after the funeral. We booked a comedy café in east London and set up an afternoon of telling Mike stories. There was music, much laughing and crying and it was as if he was there with us enjoying the day. We had produced the Harskin Papers which collected together some of Mike's best stories in the media whether they were for the Young Liberals, the Brent Liberals as a Counselor or as editor of *Liberal News*. Our retrospective included:

*"Sunday 18 February 1990, woke up at 2pm [the usual time for Mike-- editor] just in time to see Michelle's latest traumas in EastEnders. Had wonderful plans for today, but slept through most of them! Instead tidied up the bedroom, wrote another 100 envelopes and generally pottered around, staying up too late and drinking too many cups of tea and coffee."* (Harskin, 1990)

Simon Hughes, MP, came to the memorial at the comedy café and spoke, as did Vincent Hanna by now a former Newsnight BBC correspondent. Hanna was supposed to be at a G7 meeting in Birmingham helping the government with the media for the event. He spoke of his moments with Mike:

*"I asked why the YLs and not the Young Socialists – 'they always have a true faith, an orthodoxy, against which some group are constantly in schism. And everyone knows that half believers are far worse than complete heretics' [he said]. I met Mike at by-elections.*

He was one of the celebrated notorious crew, whom David Steel said didn't exist, who inhabited the neither regions of the Party office.

"[Mike was an integral part of the] tiny crew who slept under photo-copiers and produced propaganda. It was dramatic stuff, scurrilous, offensive, acerbic, funny, unfair, occasionally half true or untrue, and it terrified the other parties to death.

"I thought it was wonderful. Here were two great Party machines with offset printers clacking away, with glossy posters by the mile, highly paid staff, flashy cars, being driven rat-arsed by three Liberals with a letraset, a photocopier, a typewriter and a pot of paste.

"And Harskin was the worst. Peter Chegwyn said to me: "He's talented Mike, you know but he goes a bit over the top.

"In short, Mike Harskin was the most honorable of British political things, a pamphleteer……

"We live - relatively speaking – in a decent and humane society. People are not often imprisoned without a trial or arbitrarily executed. The opposition we see comes neatly packaged from government ministers and state torture is usually accompanied by redundancy payments.

"But in many other countries of the world you will find Mike Harskin. He'll be living in some safe house, or keeping one jump ahead of the security police, or sharing a prison cell with a trade union leader or an outspoken priest.

"Without the Mike Harskins of this world, or the next, opposition would be just a little bit more deep-rooted, and injustice more widespread.

"Mike Harskin took and gave no more – in the struggle. But nowadays that is edge is all you can have – the difference between night and day, or life or death." (Hanna, 1992)

I wonder what Mike would say about the Trump era and "fake news" I like to think he would be at the forefront of challenging it…but perhaps only after lunch each day.

# Chapter 6

# Thirty-Five Years since the Emergence of the *Green Guard* in the Liberal Party

*"This world demands the qualities of youth; not a time of life but a state of mind, a temper of the will, a quality of the imagination, a predominance of courage over timidity, of the appetite for adventure over the life of ease." Bobby Kennedy*

**Thirty-Five Years since the Emergence of the *Green Guard* in the Liberal Party**

Published in December 2017 in the Green Liberal Democrat Magazine Challenge

## Introduction

A number of the *Green Guard* got together in late November to remember one of our fallen comrades; Mike Harskin who died in 1992; but who was at the centre of a wave of new young liberals who wanted to green the Liberal Party.

Thirty-five years after the *Green Guard* came on to the scene its perhaps a good time to review their impact.

## Red Guard

There have been two times where the Young Liberals have played a critical role in the philosophical direction of the Party. The first was of course the Red Guard period from the 1960s to the early 1970s. Gaining the name after sponsoring the anti-NATO resolution at the 1966 Party conference.

The leader Jeremy Thorpe was so worried about the activities of the youth wing that he set up a three-man commission. They produced the Terrell Report which accused some of the Young Liberals of being communists (*hence the Maoist "Red Guard" epithet*). At the time and during the *Green Guard* period many Young Liberals described themselves as "libertarian socialists". Best expressed by former YL Chair Peter Hain and future Labour Cabinet Minister:

*"Underlying libertarian socialism is a different and distinct notion of politics which rests on the belief that it is only through interaction with others in political activity and civic action that individuals will fully realise their humanity. Democracy should therefore extend not simply to government but throughout society: in industry, in the neighbourhood or in any arrangement by which people organise their lives."*

Mike Harskin`s version of this was:

*"Liberalism is a rich cocktail of anarchism, socialism with a green strand"* (1985)

Another group of Young Liberals led by Bernard Greaves, Tony Greaves , Gordon Lishman and David Penhaligon developed a theory that combined a radical YL approach and drew from the US Students for a Democratic Society`s ideas on participatory democracy. The idea was to actively engage in their communities. The Young Liberals amended the Party's strategy at the Liberal Party Conference in Eastbourne in 1970; an amendment which was passed with little enthusiasm from the Party leadership. The amendment defined the new strategy as:

*"a dual approach to politics, acting both inside and outside the institutions of the political establishment to help organise people in their communities to take and use power to build a Liberal power-base in the major cities of this country to identify with the under-privileged in this country and the world to capture people's imagination as a credible political movement, with local roots and local successes."*

This was to revolutionize the Party – it became known as "community politics".

### Green Guard

The Liberal Party had adopted a no-growth economic strategy in 1979 which took into consideration the impacts of the economy on the environment. This was a beacon for the growing environment activism that had been birthed with the moon landing and the UN Conference in 1972 on Human Environment. By 1982 young people were looking for a political Party that took the environment seriously and the Liberal Party looked like it would be a good place to have some impact. The Alliance with the Social Democratic Party (SDP) had shot them to what at the time looked like a possible government with opinion polls showing them on over 50%.

The *Green Guard*, like the *Red Guard*, also focused on foreign policy issues such as Cruise missiles and Trident. One of the successes of those years was to ensure that the Party kept to its 'Liberal Values on Defence and Disarmament' engineering the coalition that beat the Party leadership on defence at the 1986 Party conference. It published a booklet of the same name. This resulted in a major defeat of the Party's attempt to go against long held views and more importantly values that the Party stood for. The conference vote backed the rebels by twenty-three votes (652 votes to 625). Many believe that the speech by Simon Hughes, one of the three MP who backed the YL push, won the day for the rebels:

*"Fellow Liberals, we could change the direction of British defence and disarmament policy. But we are a Party. Many of us joined this Party because of its aim and its goal: a non-nuclear Europe in a non-nuclear world. We have never voted to replace independent nuclear deterrent. Not only must we not do so now, but our policy must be to do so never – and, to replace an independent British nuclear deterrent by a European nuclear deterrent - even if that concept was workable - is not an acceptable alternative.... We are on the verge of responsibility. There's no more important subject - the battle is not between us, the battle is for our future. I urge you to accept both amendments and the resolution and be proud of all that we stand for.* [applause; standing ovation] "

The approach of the 1980 YLs, like their predecessors the Red Guard, pushed for *active* green policies at the local level with Liberal Councils across the country leading the way on tackling CFC recycling to protect the ozone layer, greening our towns with more cycle paths and attacking local water and air pollution challenges. At the national level, MPs like Simon Hughes, David Alton, Michael Meadowcroft and David Penhaligon in particular, led the push in parliament for green policies. Some *Green Guard* members would, themselves, become MPs in the 2000s - Adrian Sanders and Martin Horwood.

The 1980s put the YLs in coalition with Greenpeace, Friends of the Earth and other environmental groups. Des Wilson, who had been President of Friends of the Earth, became the Party President and election coordinator for the 1987 General Election. It was as if we were the Green Party. We were one of the first groups to address the issue of climate change seriously. We were also at the forefront in addressing a rights agenda whether it was the problems in Northern Ireland, gay and women's rights or the need to fund international development.

## Thirty-five years later

Looking at the state of the world in 2017 it is clearer where the successes were and where we did not address key issues which we should have done.

Perhaps we should view the bad news first. We had no economic experts or proper theory on how or what the real elements of a green economic policy was or wasn't. We weren't alone in the Party or in the greater green movement. David Boyle and others have constantly reminded Liberal Democrats that we need a real economic conversation and education. This seems strange, considering the impact that the Liberal Party of the 1930s had on 20th century economic policy with Keynes and Beveridge.

If there has been any push on economics in the Party, it has been from the right of the Party and that has not represented the values and principles that the Liberal Party upheld throughout the 20th century as Beveridge says:

*"liberals believe our guiding force should not be self-interest, class conflict, but the determination not to rest while any are condemned to want, disease, ignorance and unemployment."*

Pretty good! I would add to the end `or an unsustainable planet`.

The Liberal Democrats predicted the economic crisis but DID not do enough while in government to break up the financial casino capitalism that still is in control of the markets. I said this in at a UN conference I was chairing in 2011:

*"In the same way that banks succeeded at privatizing the profits and socializing the losses as they led the global economy to the brink of collapse, we are in danger of doing the same with the environment. Humanity has taken a huge leap in the last decades and become a planetary-scale force - we need to behave as a global civilization if we are not to face catastrophic consequences."*

We should have sent the bankers to jail – as happened in Ireland and Iceland. This has fed the rise of economic nationalism and can be tied back to that and we did NOT voice or act on that concern enough. The Labour leader has now been seen as the true advocate of accountability and it should have been US. The next financial crisis is not far away it happens roughly every 10 years in one form or another. Are we prepared? No!

On Iraq, the Party took the principled position on the war was illegal and needed a second resolution, I would point out so, behind the scenes, did most of the former Major cabinet.

On the issue of nuclear power and weapons the Party has now taken policies that would not fit in with the *Green Guard* perspective. It is very difficult to understand why that is - there is no evidence that nuclear power has a role in our energy mix and with the costs of renewables already competitive and getting more by the day then I believe this is a misstep.

Nowadays I spend most of my time at UN meetings where I have seen the UK reputation and impact decrease significantly over the last ten years - we are no longer a major power in most discussions. That we have nuclear weapons is the only reason that we are taken account of on peace and security now.

Where the UK used to lead on environmental issues, France and Germany have that role as well as leading developing countries such as Brazil, South Africa, Colombia and India and China.

On the positive side the Party is still working at the local level to promote green policies and the UK Green Bank could have been a real significant partner in this. But it has recently been sold off by the Conservatives! The Party has been at the forefront of the climate change issue on the successful push for 0.7% of GNI for development aid.

## The Future

If the *Green Guard* were to come along today, these are the areas I believe they and the Party need to have coherent policies in line with the enhanced Beveridge quote above on:

1. Climate Change and energy policy to keep within the 2-degree C target. Liberal Democrat Councils set CO2 targets to lead the way. (*unsustainable planet*);

2. An economic policy for 2030 and 2050 not one for 2020 – we can no longer in the future base taxation on income (*unsustainable planet, want and self-interest*);

3. A dialogue on the impact of new technologies and what policies are needed to address them (*employment*);

4. Regulation of the finance sector and companies to ensure they 'do no harm' in the environment – this would include companies required to produce their Environment-Social and Governance reports like they produce their economic reports to be listed on stock exchanges (*unsustainable planet and self-interest*);

5. A return to free higher education like German has done (*ignorance*)

6. A health service focusing on prevention and by doing that taking on fast foods and 'bad foods' (*want, ignorance*)

7. Adopt a rights-based approach dealing with welfare, wellbeing and environmental issues *(ignorance, want, self-interest, unsustainable planet)*

8. Set up an Ombudsman for Future Generations *(unsustainable planet)*

9. Support the establishment of an International Court on the Environment *(unsustainable planet)*

10. Address the issue of migration and refugees as Beveridge would have done *(self-interest, want, ignorance)*

We live in perhaps the most insure world since the 1960s and what we need is inspiring leadership that understands the risks and challenges ahead. The Liberal Democrats have been at the forefront of flagging up the Economic Crisis in 2007 and the challenges of economic nationalism as expressed by Trump and Brexit. Climate change is a great equalizer - we all will be impacted by it over the coming years and having a President in the White House who doesn't accept science, and promotes fake news, creates an even more *'Clear and Present Danger'* to us all.

I hope this reflection sparks some conversations in the Party and beyond. The YLs of the Red and *Green Guard* period were successful because they reached outside of the Party to bring new ideas and people into the Party but ultimately, they worked for the promotion of liberalism as opposed to the Party. You can find liberals in all parties and that is why at the end of the *Green Guard* we produced the book *'Into the 21st Century: An Agenda for political Realignment'* (1988 still available on Amazon) in which we argued we need to work on green and liberal issues **across the parties together. An earlier echo of the talk of progressive alliances that are on the table now. By working together, we can create the just, equitable, fair and sustainable planet that would be the achievement of liberals.**

# Chapter 7
# Afterword

*"As long as poverty, injustice and gross inequality persist in our world, none of us can truly rest."* Nelson Mandela

You might ask yourself what did those in this story find themselves doing in the last thirty-five years. Did they continue to work to change the world?

Many of them did but not stay active in the Liberal Democrats after the Young Liberals. The Young Liberals had become a place for radicals some of which weren't interested so much in the parliamentary side of being a member of the youth wing of the Liberal Party. Some have added to the political debate since they left in NGOs or in the media. A surprising number have continued to contribute to the political discourse through publishing books on sustainable development, realignment of British Politics, Foreign and Security Policy, Democracy, Electoral System. LGBT Rights, Ghosts, Poems, the Alliance (SDP-Liberal) and guides on how to engage in the intergovernmental process.

**Felix Dodds** my journey took me to be the Executive Director of Stakeholder Forum for a Sustainable Future for twenty years helping to increase the access of stakeholders to intergovernmental negotiations. Also contributing often through my writings to the ideas around environmental security, governance and the history of the multilateral negotiations around sustainable development. My books are:

- **Santa's Green Christmas:  Father Christmas battles Climate Change,** Dodds, F. Strauss, M. and Charles, J. New York, Comics Uniting Nations, 2016
- **Negotiating the Sustainable Development Goals: A transformational agenda for an insecure world** Dodds, F., Leiva Roesch, J. and Donoghue, D. Ambassador, London, Routledge, 2016
- **Governance for Sustainable Development** Luna, S., Lim, H., Rebedea, O., Banisar, D., Dodds, F. and McKew, Q edited, Apex, New World Frontiers, 2015
- **Plain Language Guide to Rio+20 and the New Development Agenda**, Dodds, F., Celis Laguna, J. and Thompson, L. Apex, New World Frontiers, 2014
- **From Rio+20 to a New Development Agenda: Building a Bridge to a Sustainable Future,** Dodds, F., Celis Laguna, J. and Thompson, L. London, Routledge – Earthscan, 2014
- **Only One Earth- The Long Road via Rio to Sustainable Development,** Dodds, F. Strauss, M. Strong, M. London Routledge - Earthscan, 2012
- **Biodiversity and Ecosystem Insecurity A Planet in Peril,** edited Djoghlaf, A. Dodds, F., London Earthscan, 2011
- **Climate and Energy Insecurity**, Dodds, F. Higham, H, Sherman, R., edited London, Earthscan, 2009
- **Negotiating and Implementing MEAs: A Manual for NGOs,** Dodds, F, Strauss, Howell, M, Onestini, M., Nairobi, UNEP, 2007

- **Environment and Human Security – An Agenda for Change**, edited Dodds, F and Pippard, T., London Earthscan, 2005
- **Strauss How to Lobby at Intergovernmental Meetings or Mine is a Café Latte**, Dodds, F (with Michael, London, Earthscan, 2004
- **Earth Summit 2002 - A New Deal,** edited Dodds, F., London. Earthscan 2000
- **The Way Foreword Beyond Agenda 21** edited, Dodds, F., London. Earthscan, 1997
- **Into the Twenty First Century – An Agenda for Political Realignment** Dodds, F., London. Earthscan, 1988

**Stephen Grey** one of the leading lights of the greens in the YLs became a war journalist for the Sunday Times and an investigative journalist for Reuters. Best known for revealing details of the CIA's program of 'extraordinary rendition.'. He has also reported extensively from the conflicts in Iraq and Afghanistan. 2005 he received the Amnesty International UK Media Award for best article in a periodical for his New Statesman article the American Gulag. In 2006, he received the Joe and Laurie Dine award for Best International Reporting in any medium dealing with human rights from the Overseas Press Club of America. He has become an author of a number of bestselling books:

- **The New Spymasters: Inside the Modern World of Espionage from the Cold War to Global Terror.** New York: St. Martin's Press, 2015
- **Into the Viper's Nest: The First Pivotal Battle of the Afghan War**, London, Zenith Press, 2010
- **Operation Snakebite: The Explosive True Story of an Afghan Desert Siege.** London: Viking Penguin, 2009.
- **Ghost Plane: The True Story of the CIA Torture Program**. New York: St. Martin's Press, 2006.

**Edward Lucas** became a senior editor at The Economist he is also a senior vice-president at the Centre for European Policy Analysis (CEPA). He writes a weekly column in the London Times. He worked as a foreign correspondent in Berlin, Prague, Vienna, Moscow and the Baltic States. He worked for the BBC and the Sunday Times. He founded the English language weekly in Tallinn Estonia: the Baltic Independent. He is also a author with bestselling books:

- **Cyberphobia: reveals the ways in which cyberspace is not the secure zone we may hope**, London, Bloomsbury Publishing, 2015
- **The New Cold War: Putin's Threat to Russia and the West,** London, Bloomsbury Publishing, 2014

- **Snowden Operation, London,** Amazon Crossing, 2014
- **Deception: Spies, Lies and How Russia Dupes the West**, London, Bloomsbury Publishing, 2013

**Andrew Reynolds** is a lecturer at University of North Carolina. His research and teaching focus on democratization, constitutional design and electoral politics. He is particularly interested in the presence and impact of minorities and marginalized communities. He has worked for the United Nations, the International Institute for Democracy and Electoral Assistance (IDEA), the UK Department for International Development, the US State Department, the National Democratic Institute, the International Republican Institute, the Organization for Security and Cooperation in Europe (OSCE) and the International Foundation for Election Systems

- **The Children of Harvey Milk,** Chapel Hill, Oxford University Press USA, 2018
- **The Arab Spring** (with Jason Brownlee and Tarek Masoud), Chapel Hill, Oxford University Press – USA, 2016
- **Designing Democracy in a Dangerous World**. Chapel Hill, Oxford University Press - USA, 2011
- **Electoral System Design: The New International IDEA Handbook**, London, International Idea, 2005
- **The Architecture of Democracy: Constitutional Design, Conflict Management, and Democracy,** Chapel Hill, Oxford University Press – USA, 2002
- **Election '99 South Africa: From Mandela to Mbeki,** London, Palgrave MacMillan, 2000
- **Electoral Systems and Democratization in Southern Africa,** London, Oxford University Press – USA, 1999
- **Elections and Conflict Management in Africa**, co-edited with T. Sisk, United States Institute for Peace

**Kieran Seale** has focused his work on improving public services working for the public and private sector.

- **Informal Urban Street Markets: International Perspectives,** edited Kieran Seale and Clifton Evans, London Routledge, 2015

**Rachael Pitchford (Vasmer)** with Tony Greaves. Rachael is a Salaried Judge of the First-tier Tribunal, Social Entitlement Chamber. Her main contribution has been a book with Tony Greaves on what happened in the Merger between the Liberals and the Social Democratic Party.

- **Merger - The Inside Story**, London Liberal Renewal, 1989

Outside of the political discourse a couple of the YLS have written other books.

**Rosie Dodds** went on to work at the National Childbirth Trust and co-authored

- **Safe Food: What to Eat and Drink in Pregnancy (National Childbirth Trust Guides),** with Hannah Hulme Hunter, Thorsons, 1999

**John Fraser took** a different path after the Young Liberals engaging as a member of the governing body of the Society for Psychical Research and Vice Chair of the Ghost Club. His only book so far is:

- **Ghost Hunting: A Survivors Guide,** London, The History Press, 2010

**Noel Nowosielski** runs a coaching consultancy service for the general public and the Social Care sector. His writing has focused on poetry and are:

- **Czech Out the Ladies'**, London, Babbling Bard Publications, 1996
- **Where Did I Leave My Heart?** London, Babbling Bard Publications, 2000

**Dylan Harris** has been prolific in books that are poetry or visual image most with a political focus. He also writes a regular blog all can be found at https://dylanharris.org. He describes himself as an arts voyager putting out poetry, photographs and music. His publications are:

- **Big Town Blues**, Knives Forks and Spoons Press, 2018
- **Brexit: a study of corruption,** Corrupt Press, 2017
- **We print the truth,** Corrupt Press, 2017
- **None of the Above,** Corrupt Press, 2017
- **Anticipating the Metaverse**, Knives Forks and Spoons Press, 2014
- **The liberation of [placeholder],** Knives Forks and Spoons Press, 2012
- **La Defence,** Corrupt Press, 2012
- **Plein,** Corrupt Press, 2012
- **The Smoke,** The Knives, Forks & Spoons Press, 2010
- **Antwerp,** Wurm Press, 2009
- **Europe,** Wurm Press

Others shave worked in the media **Carina Trimingham** working at Sky covering the OJ Simpson trial and **Andrew Harrison** at London Weekend Television. Still others became MPs **Martin Horwood and Adrian Sanders** and one a Baronesses, **Olly Grender,** who was also the Liberal Democrats Communication Director Officer and a regular on TV as a Liberal Democrat commentator.

Others stayed in local politics **Mike Cooper** as leader of Sutton Council, **Louise Harris/Bloom** as a Greater London Council member and chair of the Environment Committee at Eastleigh Council, **Graem Peter** as a Councillor on Bromley Council and **Mike Hamill** as a Councillor on Harrow Council. **Paul Wiggin** stayed with the rump of the Liberal Party that did not merge with the SDP served as Liberal councillor on Peterborough City Council.

**Not bad for a that generation of Young Liberals.**

# References

Across the Divide (1986) Across the Divide, Liberal Challenge Number 8, Liberal Party Publication, London

Alinski, S. (1971) Rules for Radicals, London, Vintage Books

Alton (1985) Speech to the House of Commons in favour of a Youth Charter

Alton, D. (1992) comments on Mike Harskin for Memorial Service, Asgard Harskin Papers

Ashdown, P. (1986) Speech to Liberal Party Assembly on Defence

Ashdown, P. (1992) letter about Author

Association of Liberal Councillors (1981) Community Politics, Hebden Bridge, ALC

Ayers, I. (1978) Election leaflet for Felix Dodds for President, Guildford, Felix Dodds papers

Beveridge, W. (1928) Yellow Book, London, Liberal Party

Campaign Briefing (1985) Issue 1 on N.V.D.C. and Youth Action

Dodds, F. (1976) Speech to Hertfordshire Young Liberals available through Felix Dodds papers

Dodds, F. and Gunner, J. (1982) Lebanon a Human Tragedy, London, Young Liberal News

Dodds, F. (1982) Egypt Country Profile, Oxford New Internationalist

Dodds, F. (1983) What is Libertarian Socialism in Young Liberal News July 1983, London NLYL

Dodds, F. and Harskin, M, (1983) Social Democracy in Young Liberal news Christmas Issue, London NLYL

Dodds, F. (1983) Anarchy! In Young Liberal News November 1983, London NLYL

Dodds, F. (1987) Liberalism in the 1990s, London Young Liberal News

Dodds, F. (1987 The new Left: A Liberal Catalyst, London, New Statesman

Dodds, F. (1988) Across the Divide, Oxford, Green Line

Dodds, F. (2011) Speech to the UN Conference Sustainable Societies: Responsive Citizens, Bonn, UN

Dodds, F. (2017) Thirty-Five Years since the Emergence of the *Green Guard* in the Liberal Party, Challenge, Green Liberal Democrats

Finkelstein, D (1984) Open Letter to YL News in Young Liberal News September 1984, London NLYL

Gladstone, W (1866) The difference between liberals and conservatives. Available online at: https://www.amazon.com/Liberalism-trust-people-temp-Gladstone/dp/B01LZ5ZDAO

Greaves, T. (2017) In the Gutter Seeing Stars, in Liberator issue 385, London, Liberator

Grimond (1966) Speech to Party Conference, London, Liberal Party

Guardian (1986) Editorial, London, Guardian

Hanna, V. (1992) Comments at Mike Harskin's Memorial

Harskin, M. (1988) New Society, London, New Society.

Harskin, M. (1990) Mike Harskin notes

Hain, P. (1988) Rallying to the red-green flag, Manchester, Guardian

Hamill, M. (1984) Steel at centre of Irish row in Conference Special Young Liberal News, April 1984, London, NLYL

Hughes, S. (1986) Speech to Liberal Party Assembly on Defence, Eastbourne,

Hughes, S. (1988) Speech to Green Voice Conference at LSE, London, Green Voice

Kennedy, E. (1980) Conference Speech, Bournemouth, Labour Party

Kennedy, F., J. (1961) Inaugural Speech for President of the United States, Washington DC, US Government

Kennedy, R. (1968) Speech on the campaign trail,

Kinnock, N (1985) Speech to Labour Party Conference, Bournemouth, Labour Party

Liberal News (1988) Into the 21$^{st}$ century, London, Liberal news

Liberal Party (1970 Party Conference Resolution on Community Politics and the Dual Approach to politics, London, Liberal Party

Liberal Party (1979) Liberal Party Manifesto, London, Liberal Party

Liberal Party (1980) Conference resolution on Cruise Missiles

Liberal Party (1979) Liberal manifesto, London, Liberal Party

McGiven, A. (1981) letter to the author

New Directions (1984) *Green Guard* Editorial, London, Asgard

New Directions (1984) Yippie Manifesto, London, Asgard

New Musical Express (1987) Letters Page exchange between Carina Trimingham and Steven Wells, London, NME

NLYL (1971) Scarborough Perspectives, London, NLYL

NLYL (1983) Election Leaflets, London, NLYL

NLYL (1983) Women, London, London, NLYL

NLYL (1984) Conference Motion Working for the Greens, London, NLYL

NLYL (1986) Drugs Pack, London, NLYL

North, R. (1987) Greens prepare to woo grassroots Liberals, London, The Independent

O'Callaghan, P. (1984) Troops Out in Conference Special Young Liberal News, April 1984, London, NLYL

Oza, J. (1983) Analysis of Racism in Young Liberal News July 1983, London, NLYL

Penhaligon, D. (1984) comments on nuclear weapons, Party Conference Speech, Liberal Party

Rawnsley, A. (1988) article on David Steel finishing as the leader of the Liberal Party

Robinson, T. (1978) UP Against the Wall, London, Robinson

Rogers, B. (1986) London, The Times

Social and Liberal Democrat Party (1981) Lime House Statement, London, SDP

Senior (1986) Election Manifesto, London, NLYL

Senior (1987) Who put the mouth in Yarmouth? London, Liberator

Smith, C. (1984) Speech at a Gay Right Rally in Rugby

Steel (1981) Leadership speech to the Liberal Party Conference, Llandudno, Liberal Party

Steel, D. (1983) Christmas Message to the Young Liberals in Young Liberal news Christmas Issue, London NLYL

Steel, D. (1984) Steel Meetings Young Liberals in Conference Special Young Liberal News, April 1984, London, NLYL

Strawbs (1973) Part of the Union, London, A&M

Tatchell, P. (2006) comments about Simon Hughes on the radio,

The Independent (1987) Young Liberals in a Labour Alliance Friday 15th May, London, The Independent

Thompson, H., S. (1972)  Fear in Loathing on the Campaign Trail, New York, Grand Central Publishing

Voster, J. (1970) Basil D'Oliveira: The man who took on South Africa's apartheid regime, Atalanta, CNN. Available on the web site: CNN site http://www.cnn.com/2013/03/08/sport/cricket-basil-doliveira-apartheid-south-africa/index.html

Wells, S. (1987 Lib Sprog Fest!, London, New Musical Express

Wikipedia (2017) Punk Ideologies

Wilson, D. (1986) Letter to author

Wilson, D. (1987) Battle for Power, London, Sphere

University of Surrey (2008) History of the University of Surrey, Guildford, University of Surrey

Younger, S. (1982) Speech to YL Conference Western-super-mare, London, NLYL

Younger, S (1983) Fighting for Tomorrow in Young Liberal News Conference Special Easter 1983, London, NYLY

Young Liberal News (1981) Draw Results, London, NLYL

Young Liberal News (1983) Editorial November 1983, London, NLYL

Young Liberal News (1983) Party Council in Young Liberal news Christmas Issue, London NLYL

Young Liberal News (1985) Young People Involved in politics – Carshalton North ward election, in Young Liberal News April 1985, London, NLYL

# Annex 1: The Limehouse Declaration

"The progressive decay of the independence of the Labour Party, in the face of increased trade union involvement in all areas of Party policy and mechanism, has culminated in a catastrophic Wembley conference. As a result of this conference, the leadership of the Labour Party is now to be decided by a handful of trade union leaders in a smoke-filled room. This is the final straw for a Party which has been set on this course for the last twenty years. From the actions of the militant tendency, to the accusations of corruption from former Labour MPs such as Milne (1976) – it is now apparent that Labour is no longer a Party committed to parliamentary government.

In light of these changes, we propose in this document to begin a new force in the British polity. Ours will be a Council of Social Democracy – with a commitment to rally and represent all Britons who still hold the aforementioned principle of social democracy.

Ours will aim to create a society where no Briton will suffer discrimination based on issues of gender, race, religion, disability or sexuality. (full text in Annex 1)

Ours will support a radical change within society – but only with a sense of direction and stability applied, of which there is a lack in the extreme agendas of the two established political parties.

Ours will build a caring society which focuses on the power of the individual within the community. Ours will focus on a strong public sector and a strong private sector, working together to deliver the best for Britain.

Ours, with the previous goal in mind, supports an economy which gives equal support to both the public sector and the private sector – without the frequent frontier changes based on whether the far-left or far-right political Party is in power at the time. Ours will favour competitive public enterprise, co-operative ventures and profit sharing. Ours will also seek the complete elimination of poverty within Britain, without hindering free enterprise with bureaucracy imposed from the centre. Britain must harness the strength of a competitive economy, whilst ensuring a fair distribution of its rewards.

Ours wishes to see decentralisation brought to the British political system – with a special focus on how decisions are made in both industrial and governmental issues. This must be combined with efficient and practical democracy from local councils through to Westminster.

Ours does not believe that the mass unemployment we find in modern Britain is an acceptable or inevitable circumstance when pursuing economic reform. The examples set by nations such as Norway and Switzerland show that it is possible to combine social democratic government, low inflation, and high employment.

Ours will strive for Britain to be shed of all isolationist and xenophobic attitudes towards the management of our nation's foreign affairs. Hence, we support Britain's responsibilities within the European Economic Community, North Atlantic Treaty Organisation, the United Nations, and the Commonwealth. Ours will commit Britain to become a constructive and progressive force within these trans-national bodies – in order to meet the challenges faced by the modern global community, such as arms control and third world poverty. We whole-heartedly reject the isolationist tendencies which dominate the Labour Party today.

Ours shall be the Social Democratic Party (SDP). This new organisation has already received the support of a number of notable figures within Labour Party politics, a list of whom will be endorsed at an early date. Our body has support of some who were previously engaged in Labour politics, but were disaffected by the aforementioned decay of Labour's values in relation to social democracy. However, ours also reaches out to those who are outside Party politics, and those who believe that Britain cannot be reformed successfully within the sterile and rigid political framework established by the present duopoly of major parties.

This declaration signifies the re-emergence of social democracy in Great Britain, and the advent of three-Party politics in the modern era. As former Labour Party members, we can appreciate that the decision which lies ahead for members of Labour may prove to be deeply painful and agonizing. Yet with bravery, knowledge and courage, the requirement for a realignment within British politics must now be faced." (SDP, 1981)

*Figure 38:  Peace Camp Daws Hill 1982*

32640312R00094

Printed in Poland
by Amazon Fulfillment
Poland Sp. z o.o., Wrocław